Brick by Brick: Dismantling the Border Between Juvenile and Adult Justice

by Jeffrey A. Butts and Ojmarrh Mitchell

Changes in juvenile law and juvenile court procedure are slowly dismantling the jurisdictional border between juvenile and criminal justice. Juvenile courts across the United States are increasingly similar to criminal courts in their method as well as in their general atmosphere. State and Federal laws are being changed to send a growing number of young offenders to criminal court where they can be tried as if they were adults. The two court systems appear to be moving toward complete convergence. Policymakers and practitioners need to be aware of the factors leading to this convergence and they should understand the effects it may have on offenders, victims, and the general community. This chapter reviews the origins of juvenile justice in the United States, summarizes the legislative and policy changes that are effectively dismantling the juvenile-criminal border, and examines research on the impact of such policies. The discussion concludes with a review of issues that should be prominent in any debate about the future viability of the juvenile-criminal boundary.

A B S T R A C T

Jeffrey A. Butts is a Senior Research Associate and Ojmarrh Mitchell is a Research Associate in the Program on Law & Behavior at the Urban Institute in Washington, D.C.

M uch of the American public and a growing number of policymakers appear to believe that the original concept of juvenile justice was flawed.[1] Public criticism of the juvenile court intensified during the last two decades of the 20th century, and many States began to abandon those aspects of juvenile justice that were once distinctly different from the criminal (adult) justice system. Many reforms were enacted in an attempt to strengthen the Nation's response to juvenile offenders, but the reforms did not curb public criticism of the juvenile court or juvenile correctional programs. In fact, repeated reforms may have further weakened the juvenile justice system and encouraged the public to view juvenile justice as something less than real justice.

Beginning with the 1899 opening of the first juvenile court in Chicago, the juvenile justice system was designed to be quite different from the criminal justice system. Juvenile courts emphasized an individualized approach. The disposition of each case was supposed to address the unique circumstances of the offender rather than simply matching sentences to offenses. The primary mission of a juvenile court was to investigate the factors that caused youths to go astray and then devise a package of sanctions and services that would set them back on the right track. The flexibility to fulfill this mission was provided by a lower standard of due process in juvenile court. Juvenile laws were separate from State criminal codes. Young offenders were brought into juvenile court for acts of "delinquency" rather than crimes. There were fewer formalities in order to free judges to intervene in whatever fashion they deemed appropriate based on factors such as the youth's family background, school performance, or anything else the judge thought to be relevant.

Criminal courts, on the other hand, emphasized due process and proportionate retribution. The goal of the criminal justice system was to determine an offender's guilt or innocence as fairly and expeditiously as possible. Detailed investigations of the offender's individual circumstances were unnecessary. The primary mission of the criminal court was to express the community's disapproval of illegal behavior with an appropriate amount of punishment for every conviction.

The clear demarcation between juvenile justice and criminal justice did not survive the juvenile court's first century. By the 1980s, there was widespread dissatisfaction with both the means and the ends of traditional juvenile justice. As with other social reform efforts, it is difficult to say whether frustration with juvenile justice was borne of faulty conceptualization or poor execution. The direction taken by justice policy, however, was unmistakable. Juvenile courts began to adopt the values and orientation of criminal courts. Many States altered their laws to reduce the confidentiality of juvenile court proceedings and juvenile court records. Most States increased the legal formalities used in juvenile court and shifted the focus of the juvenile justice process away from individual-ized intervention. Instead, juvenile courts and juvenile justice agencies began to focus on public safety and offender accountability. In addition, nearly all States enacted laws to send more youths to criminal court where they could be tried and punished as adults. In the span of a single century the American justice sys-tem had enthusiastically embraced and then largely rejected the concept of using a different legal system for crimes committed by the young.

The Origins of Juvenile Justice

The founding principles of American juvenile justice were derived largely from English common law, the system of precedents formed by accumulating cen-turies of individual court judgments. The idea that children should be held to a lower standard of criminal responsibility had a long history in English law. Children were seen as less than fully developed morally and emotionally. Thus, they could not be held accountable for illegal behaviors. At least since the 13th century, English courts exempted children from otherwise deserved sentences after finding they were "too young for punishment" (Watkins 1998, 15).

Implementation of this general principle, however, was not always reliable. The age of criminal responsibility was difficult to fix, in part because judges could not always be sure of a child's true age. Civil registration of births was not cus-tomary in England until the 17th century and not required until the early 19th century, making exact age distinctions difficult. Even if courts believed a child was under the age of criminal responsibility, lenience was not guaranteed, espe-cially if there was evidence that the child tried to conceal the crime. In 1338, one court hanged an English child under the age of 7 because he had attempted to hide from the authorities after killing a playmate. The court ruled that his effort to avoid detection proved he knew the difference between right and wrong, a critical distinction in legal thinking of the time. Another English court sentenced a 9-year-old to death in 1488 because the boy attributed his blood-stained clothes to a nosebleed, proving to the court that he knew it was wrong to have killed another child (Watkins 1998, 12–13).

By the 16th century, English courts generally set age 14 as the beginning of criminal responsibility (Polier 1989, 38). The English system of common law eventually settled on the idea that children younger than 7 were by definition incapable of criminal responsibility. Children between the ages of 7 and 13 were presumed not responsible but this presumption could be reversed with evidence of criminal intent and culpability. Upon reaching age 14, all children were fully responsible for their behavior. Even this framework, however, did not guarantee fair and proportionate treatment for children. In 1835, one

English court imposed a death sentence on a 9-year-old accused of stealing a small bottle of ink from a broken shop window (Polier 1989, 38).

The American juvenile court movement

Despite the ambiguities of English law on the question of criminal responsibility, English traditions were influential in molding the ideas of the American social reformers who established the world's first juvenile court in Chicago. State legislators in Illinois sparked the juvenile court movement by passing the Juvenile Court Act of 1899. The juvenile court law was shaped by 70 years of correctional reforms and innovative court practices in other States. For instance, New York courts had been holding trials for young defendants on separate days from trials involving adults for nearly 30 years. Illinois, however, was the first to establish a truly separate juvenile court with noncriminal jurisdiction over law violations by children (Rothman 1980; Watkins 1998).

The Juvenile Court Act of 1899 gave Illinois juvenile courts legal responsibility for any child age 15 or younger who had violated the "law of this State or any city or village ordinance" (Watkins 1998, 43). As other States began to establish juvenile courts, the upper limit of juvenile court jurisdiction was often increased to age 16 or 17. In fact, as of 1997, Illinois juvenile courts had responsibility for lawbreakers age 16 and younger (Griffin, Torbet, and Szymanski 1998, A–26). The juvenile court concept proved to be very popular (see exhibit 1). Within 5 years of the opening of Chicago's court, 11 States had established juvenile courts with legislation similar to that of Illinois. By 1927, all but two States (Maine and Wyoming) had implemented juvenile courts. By 1950, every State had joined the juvenile court movement, and the number of cases handled by juvenile courts began to grow significantly (see exhibit 2).

Juvenile courts were given an unprecedented degree of power over the lives of poor and destitute children as well as those committing crimes in the streets of the Nation's growing cities. It was not unprecedented for the justice system to intervene with children. Courts had been doing that for centuries. What was new about the juvenile court was its authority to use coercive, state-sponsored intervention *outside* the criminal law. The juvenile court's authority came from civil law, much like the government's power of involuntary hospitalization for the mentally ill. The juvenile court's quasi-civil jurisdiction allowed it to take custody of young people charged with a wide array of criminal and noncriminal behaviors, from vagrancy and running away to stealing and acts of violence. The court embodied an entirely new motive for justice system intervention, to resolve problems rather than punish wrongdoing. In 1909, Judge Julian Mack of the Chicago juvenile court explained that the purpose of his court was not to ask whether a boy had committed a "special wrong" but rather "what is he, how has

Exhibit 1. States with separate juvenile courts, 1899–1950

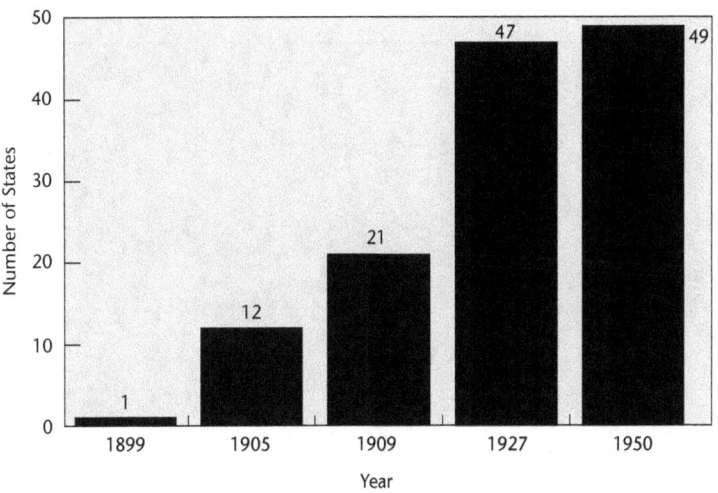

Year

Note: Illinois was the first State to establish a separate juvenile court in 1899. By 1905, 11 more States had adopted juvenile courts: California, Colorado, Indiana, Iowa, Maryland, Missouri, New Jersey, New York, Ohio, Pennsylvania, and Wisconsin. Juvenile courts were established nationwide, including Washington, D.C., by 1950.

Source: Watkins 1998, 45.

be become what he is, and what had best be done in his interest and in the interest of the state to save him from a downward career?" (Mack 1909).

The juvenile court's legal authority was drawn rather loosely from concepts in English law. The most important of these was *parens patriae*, or roughly, "nation as parent." *Parens patriae* suggested that the government had an obligation and a duty to look after the interests of children when natural parents were unable to do so. Long before the concept was discovered by American reformers, England's Chancery Courts had been invoking *parens patriae* to take temporary custody of land and property that would eventually revert to the orphaned children of wealthy families (Polier 1989, 2). In the mid-1800s, some American courts had also used *parens patriae* as a justification for placing recalcitrant children in "houses of refuge," an early form of poorhouse and reformatory (Bernard 1992). With a little creative interpretation, America's juvenile court advocates argued that *parens patriae* should allow the government to take charge of any child who was destitute, neglected, or ill-behaved.

Exhibit 2. Delinquency cases handled by U.S. juvenile courts, 1941–96

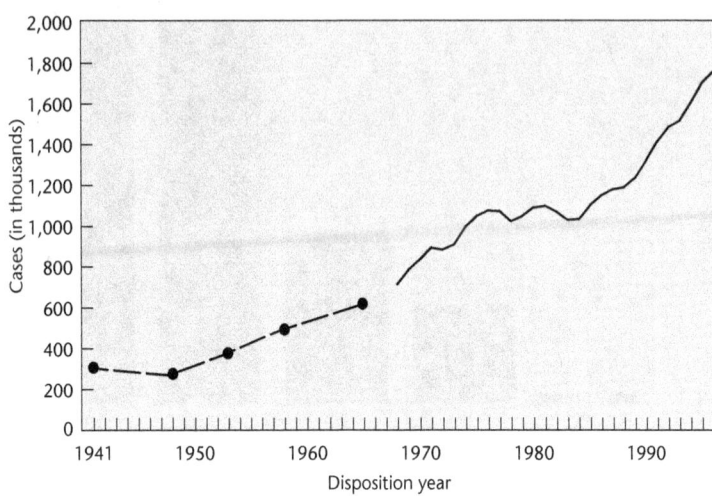

Note: Data from 1941 to 1968 are not continuous. Years represented are 1941, 1948, 1953, 1958, 1965, and 1968.

Sources: 1941–65: Manfredi 1998, 35; 1968–86: Butts 1997b; 1987–96: Stahl 1998.

The Progressive Era reformers who founded the juvenile court were also inspired by 19th-century intellectual developments in correctional techniques and the new field of social science. Juvenile court reformers were especially taken with the views of positivism that then dominated the social sciences (Feld 1999, 57). Positivism suggested that social problems such as crime and poverty were caused by factors that could be identified and corrected with the proper scientific methods. Positivism gave reformers the faith and confidence to intervene. *Parens patriae* gave them the power.

Part social services, part law enforcement

Although most contemporary accounts portray founders of the juvenile court as do-gooders and middle-class meddlers, early proponents of juvenile courts were as interested in crime control as they were in social reform (Platt 1977). Before the development of juvenile courts, young thieves and muggers appeared in criminal court alongside adult defendants. Judges and jurors frequently found young people innocent or simply released them, especially when youths were charged with nonviolent offenses and appeared socially immature. Acquittal was preferable to sending such youngsters to prison. After years of frustration with the criminal court's inability to sanction young offenders, police and prosecutors began to press for a separate juvenile court that would consider the illegal behavior of young people on its own terms (Schlossman 1977).

As their deliberations were defined as quasi-civil, juvenile courts were not required to abide by the constitutional restrictions applied to criminal prosecutions. Early juvenile courts did not have to contend with defense attorneys, appeals, or formal evidentiary procedures. Prosecutors were required to prove juvenile charges based only on a "preponderance of the evidence" rather than the far stricter standard of "beyond a reasonable doubt." In recognition of their distinct legal standing, juvenile courts developed a new vocabulary. Youths appearing in juvenile court were "delinquents" rather than defendants. They were "adjudicated" instead of being found guilty. Final decisions were "dispositions" rather than sentences. Youths held overnight were "detained" in a juvenile detention center, not jailed.

This quasi-civil legal authority endowed the juvenile court with broad discretion to intervene. Juvenile court judges were free to develop individualized and sometimes creative dispositions for young offenders. Contemporary debates often omit this feature of the juvenile court concept, but it is a critical factor in explaining why the juvenile court idea was as popular with judges and police officers as it was with social reformers. Some scholars have noted that the caseloads of early juvenile courts were dominated by minor offenses and noncriminal youths (Fox 1970). To some, this may suggest that juvenile courts were never designed to handle serious offenders. Such an analysis, however, focuses on the proportion of serious offenses among the total caseload of early juvenile courts, and it overlooks the fact that juvenile courts began as multipurpose social service centers. The juvenile court represented one of the first organized efforts to address the needs of ill-behaved, unsupervised, and neglected children outside the orphanage or the poorhouse. It is not surprising that their caseloads included large numbers of noncriminal and nonserious offenders.

Historians have found that serious offenders were always part of the juvenile court's workload (Rothman 1980). In fact, some prosecutors and police departments altered their procedures in order to send larger numbers of serious offenders to the new juvenile courts rather than keeping them in adult court. For instance, the District of Columbia enacted its first juvenile court law in 1906 and originally limited the court's jurisdiction to misdemeanors. Felony charges remained in criminal court. Prosecutors soon became frustrated that misdemeanor cases received relatively stiff sanctions in juvenile court while felony charges were often dropped because grand juries refused to return indictments against young offenders in adult court. In response, prosecutors

The informality and flexibility in juvenile court provided conscientious judges with the freedom to intervene in the lives of troubled youths.

began to modify the offenses they charged against young offenders in order to send more of them to juvenile court. A charge of felony auto theft, for example, might be reduced to the misdemeanor offense of "operating a vehicle without a permit." A study submitted to Congress in the 1920s estimated that more than half of the so-called misdemeanors handled in the District of Columbia juvenile court were actually downgraded felonies (U.S. Senate 1927, 47).

The juvenile court movement spread rapidly across the United States because it offered a new approach to handling young offenders who were often ignored in the crowded chaos of criminal court. Police and prosecutors saw the juvenile court as a way to avoid bureaucratic delays and to ensure that more young offenders were sanctioned for their crimes. Social reformers valued the new court because it was informal and personal, allowing the legal process to attend to the unique circumstances of every youth. Judges could speak with each youth brought before the court. Probation officers could make a thorough investigation of each offender's home life. Due process protections for accused youths were unnecessary because the juvenile court itself was devoted to their best interests.

An early study of the District of Columbia juvenile court noted that the Washington legal establishment supported the development of a juvenile court for several reasons. Among these were the:

> unsatisfactory atmosphere and environment of the old police court, which could be avoided only by a children's court located elsewhere; the fact that judges wearied with the "harassing cases of drunks, disorderlies," and the like, could not bring to the consideration of children's cases a calm, sympathetic attitude; a condition under which judges, presiding at alternate sessions of the court could not keep track of individual offenders or know even the court history of each case; the fact that judges handling a variety of cases could not find time to make a special study of child psychology and the special problems of a children's court. (U.S. Senate 1927, 35–36)

Reform and Retreat

Unfortunately, the informality that was so highly valued by reformers also made the juvenile court vulnerable as a legal institution. As soon as juvenile courts began to spread across the United States in the early 1900s, State and local governments began to improvise variations on the Chicago opus. A variety of court structures and procedural approaches began to develop as each jurisdiction fit the general concept of the juvenile court into its own legal and organizational culture (Rothman 1980; Sutton 1988). One State might have required its juvenile courts to follow procedures resembling those of the criminal courts, including jury trials, evidentiary motions, or formal sentencing investigations. Another State might have asked only that juvenile court judges follow their conscience in making court dispositions, a degree of discretion not found in adult trial courts. Since juveniles were not legally at risk of a criminal trial, there were fewer restrictions on the methods used in juvenile courts.

> *Judges could order a combative or emotionally disturbed youth into a group home or shelter, even if there was only vague evidence that the youth had actually committed an offense.*

This was both the best and the worst aspect of the juvenile court. The informality and flexibility in juvenile court provided conscientious judges with the freedom to intervene in the lives of troubled youths. If a youth's circumstances seemed to pose merely the risk of future criminal behavior, the court was empowered to act. Judges could order a combative or emotionally disturbed youth into a group home or shelter, even if there was only vague evidence that the youth had actually committed an offense. This provided thoughtful and compassionate judges with profound and often effective discretion.

The same freedom, however, could be abused. The length and severity of juvenile court intervention did not have to be proportional to the seriousness or dangerousness of a youth's behavior. A juvenile could be adjudicated and placed in secure confinement for relatively innocuous offenses, including swearing, smoking tobacco, and even adolescent sexual behaviors (Schlossman and Wallach 1978). If so inclined, a juvenile court judge was free to impose his or her private views of morality on young and sometimes relatively innocent youths. Even worse, the judge could punish juvenile behavior more severely when it occurred in unfamiliar cultural or racial settings (Feld 1999).

Within a few decades of the juvenile court's founding, some observers began to wonder whether the idealism of the Progressives had been excessive. Juvenile courts, especially those in urban areas, began to exhibit the worst features of criminal courts. Caseloads swelled, courtrooms fell into disrepair, and staff became disenchanted and disinterested. One juvenile court judge from New York, Justine Wise Polier, noted that by the middle of the 20th century, the juvenile court was "bowed down by disabilities imposed by law and custom on all institutions for the poor." She compared the juvenile court's hurried ambiance with the "disposition of the dead during a plague" (Polier 1989, 4).

By the 1930s and 1940s, "youth charged with offenses sat for hours in airless waiting rooms. Noisy verbal and physical battles had to be broken up by court attendants. The hard benches on which everyone was forced to sit and the atmosphere, like that in lower criminal courts, resembled bullpens more than a court for human beings" (Polier 1989, 4).

Increasingly bureaucratic and overburdened, the juvenile court system started to attract the attention of youth advocates and civil rights lawyers. During the 1950s, legal activists began to challenge the sweeping discretion given to juvenile court judges. One influential law review article published in 1957 questioned whether juvenile courts were entirely benevolent, arguing that "an adjudication of delinquency, in itself, is harmful and should not be capriciously imposed" (Paulsen 1957, 547, 569). Another article charged juvenile courts with violating important principles of equal protection and argued that "rehabilitation may be substituted for punishment, but a star chamber cannot be substituted for a trial" (Beemsterboer 1960, 464). Reform was clearly in the offing when Chief Justice Earl Warren noted in a 1964 speech to the National Council of Juvenile Court Judges that controversies over due process in the juvenile court would be resolved as soon as the "proper" case came before the U.S. Supreme Court (Manfredi 1998, 52). The proper case arrived soon thereafter from the State of Arizona.

Constitutional domestication of the juvenile court

The American juvenile justice system changed suddenly and dramatically in 1967 when the U.S. Supreme Court announced its decision in *In re Gault* (387 U.S. 1 [1967]). A few years earlier, an Arizona juvenile court judge had institutionalized 15-year-old Gerald Gault for making a mildly obscene telephone call. He was accused of asking a female neighbor several strange and obviously adolescent questions, of which the most offensive were, "Are your cherries ripe today?" and "Do you have big bombers?" (Bernard 1992, 114). Based on the neighbor's complaint, Gerald and a friend were picked up by the local Sheriff. The court did not bother to notify Gerald's family that he was in custody. It never heard testimony from the victim in the case, and it never established whether Gerald or his friend had actually made the call. Gerald was committed to a State institution for delinquent boys for the "period of his minority," or 3 years. If he had been an adult, his sentence would likely have been a small fine.

The Supreme Court's reaction to Gault's appeal was strong and far reaching. In any delinquency proceeding in which confinement was a possible outcome, the Court ruled, youths should have the right to notice of charges against them and the right to cross-examine prosecution witnesses, the right to assistance of counsel, and the protection against self-incrimination. The Court based its ruling on the fact that Gerald Gault had clearly been *punished* by the juvenile court and not *treated*. The opinion also explicitly rejected the doctrine of *parens patriae* as the founding principle of juvenile justice. The Court described the meaning of *parens patriae* as "murky" and characterized its "historic credentials" as "of dubious relevance." "The constitutional and theoretical basis for this peculiar system is—to say the least—debatable" (Bernard 1992, 116, quoting from the *Gault* opinion).

Gault was one of a series of juvenile justice cases decided by the Supreme Court in the 1960s and 1970s. Together, the cases imposed significant procedural restrictions on U.S. juvenile courts. By the 1980s, juvenile courts had been "constitutionally domesticated" (Feld 1999, 79). Juveniles charged with law violations had far more due process protections, although they were still denied the Federal rights of bail, jury trial, and speedy trial. Juvenile courts were required to follow a higher standard of evidence ("reasonable doubt" rather than "preponderance") and juvenile adjudications were considered equivalent to criminal convictions in evaluating double jeopardy claims (Bernard 1992, 108–134).

> *When juveniles are transferred to adult court, they lose their status as minor children and become legally culpable for their behavior. Transfer is often used for juveniles charged with serious and violent offenses. At least half of the youths transferred to the adult court system, however, have committed lesser offenses such as property and drug law violations.*

The consequences of constitutional domestication may not have been fully appreciated by reformers and youth advocates. As Justice Stewart warned in his dissent to *Gault*, the introduction of greater due process for juveniles may have had the unintended consequence of encouraging States to make their juvenile courts more like criminal courts:

> The inflexible restrictions that the Constitution so wisely made applicable to adversary criminal trials have no inevitable place in the proceedings of those public social agencies known as juvenile or family courts. And to impose the Court's long catalog of requirements upon juvenile proceedings in every area of the country is to invite a long step backwards into the nineteenth century. In that era there were no juvenile proceedings, and a child was tried in a conventional criminal court with all the trappings of a conventional criminal trial. So it was that a 12-year-old boy named James Guild was tried in New Jersey for killing Catharine Beakes. A jury found him guilty of murder, and he was sentenced to death by hanging. The sentence was executed. It was all very constitutional. (Justice Stewart dissenting, *In re Gault*, 387 U.S. 1, 79–80 [1967])

Legislative and Policy Initiatives

Justice Stewart's comments seemed all too prescient as the 20th century ended. For 30 years following the *Gault* decision, State legislatures across the United States continued the due process reforms endorsed by the Supreme Court. Using various tactics, lawmakers greatly limited the discretion of juvenile court judges and made the juvenile court process more evidence driven and formalized. They also sent far more juveniles directly to criminal court, effectively abolishing the juvenile court's jurisdiction over many categories of young offenders. The purposes and procedures of juvenile justice became increasingly similar to those of criminal justice. In effect, State governments (often echoing the tone of Federal policies) were slowly beginning to dismantle the legal and procedural border between juvenile justice and criminal justice. The following sections describe the policy initiatives used to accomplish this task.

Criminal court transfer

No single issue in juvenile justice has captured the attention of the public or of policymakers like criminal court transfer. Conflicts over the transfer issue represent the clearest and most direct dispute over the juvenile-criminal boundary. It is the same conflict that ensnared English courts for hundreds of years prior to the founding of the juvenile court, i.e., at what age should children be held responsible for illegal behavior, and what exceptions should be permitted? When juveniles are transferred to adult court, they lose their status as minor children and become legally culpable for their behavior. Transfer is often used for juveniles charged with serious and violent offenses. At least half of the youths transferred to the adult court system, however, have committed lesser offenses such as property and drug law violations.

The boundary between juvenile and adult court was always somewhat permeable. Some States began to transfer juveniles to adult court as early as the 1920s (e.g., Arkansas, California, Colorado, Florida, Georgia, Kentucky, North Carolina, Ohio, Oregon, and Tennessee); others permitted transfers since at least the 1940s (e.g., Delaware, Indiana, Maryland, Michigan, Nevada, New Hampshire, New Mexico, Rhode Island, South Carolina, and Utah) (Feld 1987). In the last two decades of the 20th century, however, lawmakers enacted new and expanded transfer mechanisms on an almost annual basis. Moreover, there was an increase in laws that moved entire classes of young offenders into criminal court without the involvement of juvenile court judges. Judicial authority in transfer decisions was diminished while the role of prosecutors and legislatures increased. Nonjudicial mechanisms, in fact, accounted for the vast majority of juvenile transfers during the 1990s.

Discretionary judicial waiver

The most traditional method of transferring juveniles to criminal court was discretionary judicial waiver. Judicial waiver laws allow a juvenile court judge to transfer a delinquency case to criminal court, often after establishing that the case meets certain criteria. Waiver proceedings are usually initiated by the prosecutor, who bears the burden of proof during transfer proceedings. Although the criteria for waiver vary by State, the provisions are typically based on those outlined by the U.S. Supreme Court in *Kent* v. *United States* (383 U.S. 541 [1966]). The *Kent* decision suggested that juvenile court judges should evaluate waiver petitions by considering the offender's age, instant offense, criminal history, perceived amenability to rehabilitation, and threat to the public, as well as the prosecutorial merit of the case.

In 1960, only half the States had statutory provisions for judicial waiver (Feld 1987). During the 1990s alone, virtually all States either enacted new waiver laws or expanded their existing waiver policies. For instance, Alabama, Idaho, Iowa, and Minnesota enacted laws that allow judicial waiver in any case involving a youthful offender at least 14 years of age. By 1997, all but five States (Connecticut, Massachusetts, Nebraska, New Mexico, and New York) and the District of Columbia allowed discretionary judicial waiver (Torbet and Szymanski 1998). From 1992 to 1997, 11 States lowered the age limit for waiver in at least some cases, 17 States made additional offenses eligible for waiver, and 6 States added or adjusted their criminal history provisions for discretionary waiver (Torbet et al. 1996; Torbet and Szymanski 1998).

The expansion of discretionary judicial waiver laws may have helped produce a 47-percent increase in the national number of judicially waived cases between 1987 and 1996 (Stahl 1999). During this period, the number of waived cases increased to approximately 10,000 a year, with an increase of 124 percent for drug offenses and 125 percent for person offenses. The largest share of cases waived by judges prior to 1992 involved property offenses. In 1987, for example, property offenses accounted for 55 percent of all waived cases nationwide (Stahl 1999). At that time, the probability of judicial waiver for formally charged property offenses (1.2 percent) was nearly as high as the chance of waiver in cases involving person offenses (1.9 percent) or drug offenses (1.6 percent). By 1996, only 0.8 percent of property offense cases were waived by juvenile court judges. Similarly, the chances of waiver for drug offenders fell to 1.2 percent. Thus, by 1996, judicially waived cases were more likely to involve offenses against persons (43 percent) than they were to involve either drug offenses (14 percent) or property offenses (37 percent) (see exhibit 3).

Exhibit 3. Cases judicially waived to criminal court, 1987–96

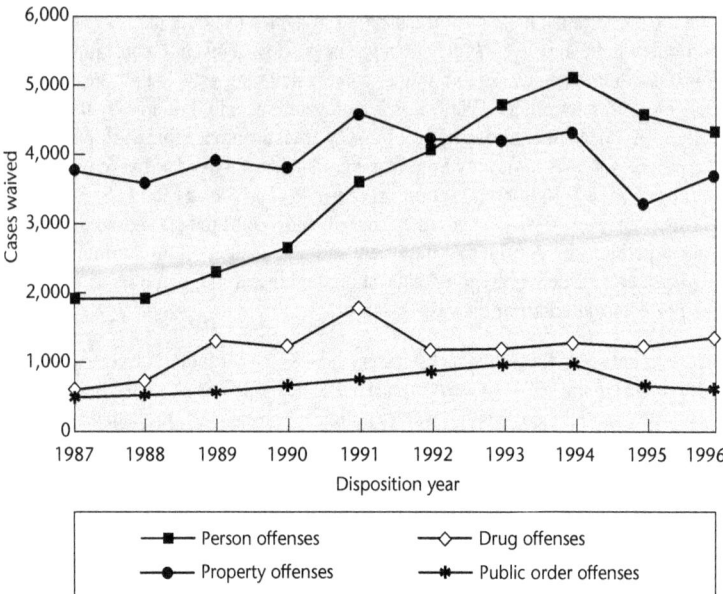

Legend:
- ■ Person offenses
- ● Property offenses
- ◇ Drug offenses
- ✳ Public order offenses

Note: Juvenile court judges waived between 1 percent and 2 percent of formally charged delinquency cases from 1987 to 1996. The number of cases waived to criminal court grew more than 70 percent between 1987 and 1994, from 6,800 to 11,700 cases annually. By 1996, the number of waived cases had declined to 10,000. Most of the increase in waived cases between 1987 and 1996 was due to the larger number of cases involving offenses against persons.

Source: Stahl 1999.

Presumptive judicial waiver

The dominant trend among State transfer laws during the 1990s was a reduction in the role of judges and a greater reliance on prosecutors. For instance, many States enacted policies that made judicial waiver "presumptive" and shifted the burden of proof from the prosecutor to the juvenile. Presumptive waiver provisions typically require a defense attorney to show proof that a youth is amenable to juvenile court disposition. Otherwise, the juvenile will be transferred to criminal court. North Dakota, for example, adopted a policy that required judges to waive any juvenile age 14 and older with two or more previous felonies and accused of committing a serious offense, unless the youth could prove he or she was amenable to rehabilitation in juvenile court (Griffin,

Torbet, and Szymanski 1998, A–57). New Jersey enacted a law that required juvenile courts only to find probable cause that public safety interests necessitated the transfer of certain juveniles age 14 and older unless the juvenile was able to argue otherwise (Griffin, Torbet, and Szymanski 1998, A–53).

There is no national information on the number of juveniles affected by these policies, but the popularity of presumptive waiver among State lawmakers certainly grew during the 1990s. Between 1992 and 1997 alone, 11 States passed new presumptive waiver provisions. Altogether, 14 States (Arizona, Arkansas, Colorado, Florida, Georgia, Louisiana, Massachusetts, Michigan, Montana, Nebraska, Oklahoma, Vermont, Virginia, and Wyoming) and the District of Columbia were known to have presumptive waiver laws by the end of the 1990s (Torbet and Szymanski 1998, 4).

Mandatory judicial waiver

Although presumptive waiver policies allow juveniles to rebut the presumption of their nonamenability to juvenile court treatment and avoid being transferred to criminal court, mandatory waiver laws provide no such escape. The juvenile court's only role in mandatory waiver proceedings is to ascertain if a particular offender meets the statutory criteria for waiver. If the juvenile meets the criteria, the juvenile court judge is left with no choice but to transfer jurisdiction of the case to criminal court. Connecticut's mandatory waiver provision, for instance, states that a defense attorney cannot make any motion or argument in opposition to criminal court transfer (Griffin, Torbet, and Szymanski 1998, 4).

There are no national data on the volume or impact of mandatory transfers, but they became far more common during the 1990s after being quite rare as recently as the 1970s. By 1997, 14 States (Connecticut, Delaware, Georgia, Illinois, Indiana, Kentucky, Louisiana, North Carolina, North Dakota, Ohio, Rhode Island, South Carolina, Virginia, and West Virginia) had enacted some form of mandatory judicial waiver (Torbet and Szymanski 1998). Typically, the criteria for mandatory transfer specified that juveniles who met various age, offense, and criminal history requirements must be transferred to criminal court. South Carolina law, for example, required juvenile court judges to transfer jurisdiction of any case involving a youth age 14 or older if the youth had been adjudicated for two or more previous offenses and was accused of an offense punishable by a sentence of at least 10 years (Griffin, Torbet, and Szymanski 1998, A–68). Indiana legislators passed a law that requires a juvenile court judge to waive *any* juvenile with a prior adjudication who is charged with a felony, regardless of the youth's age (Griffin, Torbet, and Szymanski

1998, A–28). The Indiana law used mandatory waiver to create a policy for juvenile offenders that could be described as "two strikes and you're an adult."

Statutory exclusion from juvenile court jurisdiction

The concerted expansion of judicial waiver laws and the increasingly nondiscretionary quality of transfer policies helped to weaken the border between juvenile court and criminal court during the last decades of the 20th century. Judicial waiver, however, had been available since the early days of the juvenile court movement. Other, more recent mechanisms contributed even more to the deterioration of the juvenile-adult boundary. One such mechanism that became widespread during the last years of the 20th century was statutory exclusion, known in some States as "automatic transfer."

Statutory exclusion laws mandate that certain young offenders are transferred automatically to criminal court once they are charged with certain offenses. Judicial involvement in the transfer decision is unnecessary. If a youth is at least a certain age and charged by the prosecutor with a certain offense, State law places the case directly in the criminal court's jurisdiction. Once a youth is charged with an offense statutorily excluded from juvenile court jurisdiction, the case simply bypasses juvenile court and is prosecuted in criminal court using the same procedures that would be employed in any other criminal case.

Statutory exclusion provisions vary by jurisdiction, but the criteria most commonly used to exclude cases automatically from juvenile court are combinations of age, offense, and prior record. As of 1997, for example, Georgia excluded all juveniles age 13 and older from juvenile court if they were charged with one of several violent offenses such as murder, voluntary manslaughter, rape, or armed robbery with a firearm (Griffin, Torbet, and Szymanski 1998, A–22). Arizona automatically excluded juveniles charged with any felony if the youth had been adjudicated for two or more prior felony offenses (Griffin, Torbet, and Szymanski 1998, A–8).

The popularity of statutory exclusion laws increased significantly in the 1990s. As of 1997, 28 States statutorily excluded at least some juveniles charged with certain offenses. Two States (Arizona and Minnesota) enacted new statutory exclusion provisions between 1992 and 1997, while 26 States expanded their existing statutory exclusion provisions either by lowering age limits, adding to the list of applicable offenses, or both (Torbet and Szymanski 1998, 5). Illinois lawmakers, for example, repeatedly expanded their automatic transfer statutes during the 1980s and 1990s. By 1996, the number of juveniles affected by statutory exclusion laws in Illinois far exceeded the number affected by judicial waiver (see exhibit 4).

Exhibit 4. Delinquency cases transferred to criminal court in Illinois, 1981–96

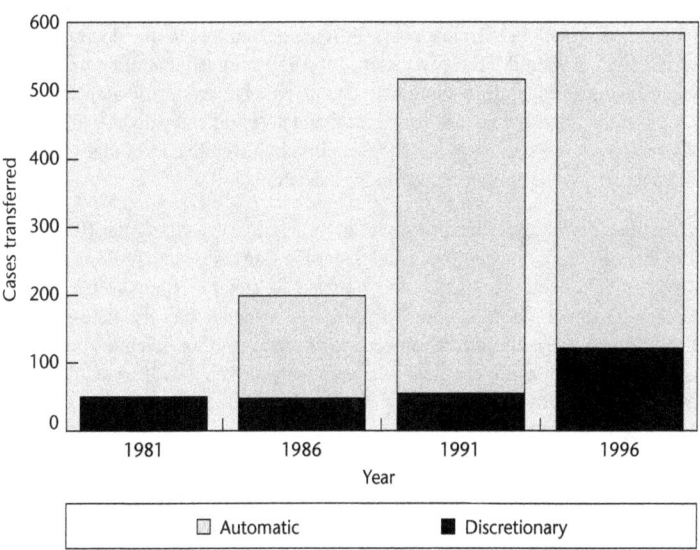

Note: A series of laws expanded the use of automatic transfer in Illinois, helping to increase the number of youths transferred to adult courts statewide.

1982: Automatic transfer statute enacted. Applied to youths age 15 and older charged with murder, rape, armed robbery, and some sexual assaults.

1985: Statute expanded to include juveniles age 15 and older charged with committing drug or weapons violations within 1,000 feet of a school.

1990: Statute expanded to include juveniles charged with felonies committed "in furtherance of gang activity."

1990: Statute expanded to include juveniles age 15 and older charged with committing drug violations within 1,000 feet of public housing.

1995: "Presumptive waiver" provision added, reducing prosecutor discretion to transfer or not to transfer certain cases.

Sources: Urban Institute analysis of data from the Administrative Office of the Illinois Courts, *Probation and court services statistical report*, Springfield, Illinois: Administrative Office of the Courts; Clarke 1996, 3–21.

Prosecutor direct filing in criminal court

Direct file, also known as concurrent jurisdiction or prosecutor discretion, is another increasingly prominent form of criminal court transfer. Direct file laws give prosecutors the discretion to prosecute juveniles either in juvenile or adult court. Judges cannot review such actions because the charging decisions of prosecutors are considered an executive function (Leeper 1991). Direct file statutes give jurisdiction over certain categories of young offenders to both the juvenile court and the criminal court. Prosecutors are free to decide in which forum a youth should face prosecution. It could be argued that other transfer mechanisms provide prosecutors with comparable powers. Prosecutor charges, for example, are often needed to trigger mandatory judicial waiver. Mandatory waivers, however, require at least some action by juvenile court judges. Direct file policies give prosecutors total independence.

The popularity of direct file provisions grew significantly during the 1980s and 1990s. In 1982, only eight States had direct file statutes (Hutzler 1982). As of 1997, 14 States and the District of Columbia had such provisions (see exhibit 5). Colorado's direct file statute, for example, was written to be very inclusive. Prosecutors were authorized to proceed in criminal court or juvenile court against any youth age 14 or older who was charged with a wide array of felony offenses, as well as any youth conspiring or attempting to commit such offenses

Exhibit 5. States (including the District of Columbia) with prosecutor direct file juvenile justice laws, 1997

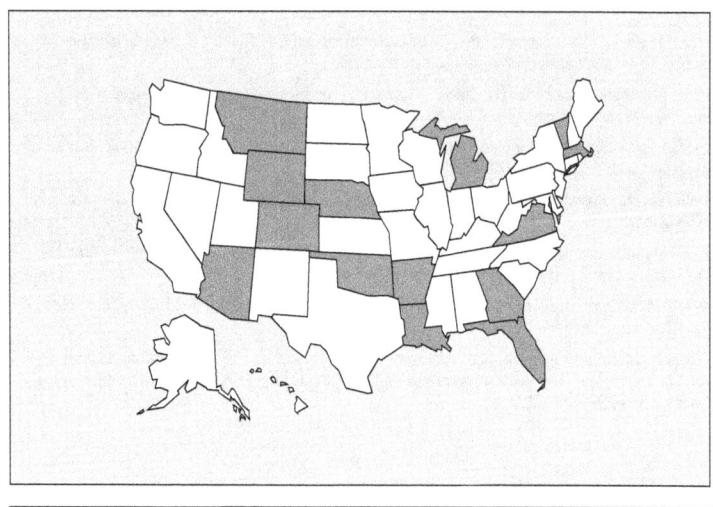

■ Allowed prosecutor direct file (15)   □ Did not allow direct file (36)

Source: Torbet and Szymanski 1998, 4.

(Griffin, Torbet, and Szymanski 1998, A–14). Louisiana adopted a direct file law that gave prosecutors discretion to file criminal charges against any youth age 15 and older who was charged with a second drug felony, a second charge of aggravated burglary, or virtually any of the Federal Bureau of Investigation's Violent Crime Index offenses (Griffin, Torbet, and Szymanski 1998, A–34).

National data about the volume of prosecutor transfers do not exist. In States that provide for such transfers, however, they are likely to greatly outnumber judicial waivers. The State of Florida significantly expanded its direct file statute in 1981, giving State's attorneys more discretion to file criminal charges against offenders younger than 18. Within a decade, the number of transfers to criminal court tripled, and transfers by prosecutors soon outnumbered judicial waivers by a margin of six to one (Snyder and Sickmund 1995, 156). In 1982, one study estimated that prosecutors nationwide transferred 2,000 cases annually (Hamparian et al. 1982). By the mid-1990s, Florida prosecutors alone transferred more than 7,000 criminal cases involving offenders under the age of 18 (see exhibit 6).

Exhibit 6. Prosecutor transfers in Florida and judicial waivers nationwide

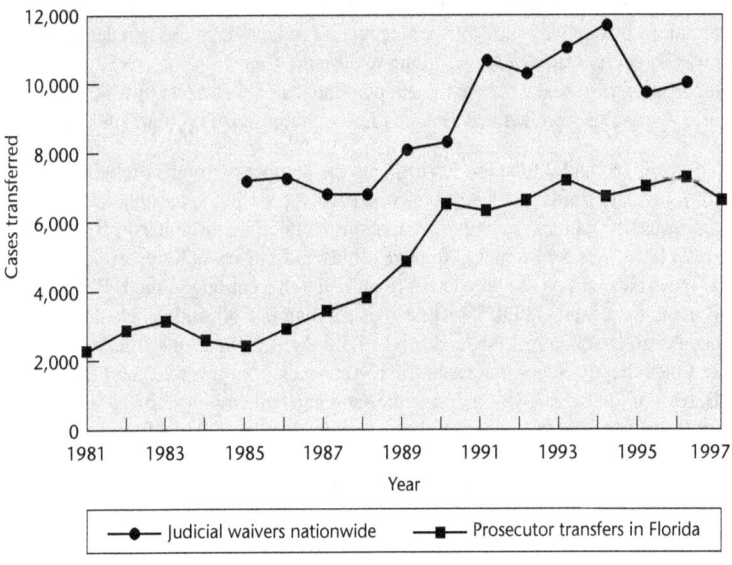

Sources: Urban Institute analysis of data from *Profile of delinquency cases and youths referred,* Bureau of Research and Data, Florida Department of Juvenile Justice; Snyder et al. 1998.

Reductions in the age of juvenile court jurisdiction

The most straightforward method of increasing the number of young offenders sent to criminal court is simply to lower the upper age of original juvenile court jurisdiction. One change in State law sends a whole cohort of arguably "juvenile" offenders into the auspices of the criminal court, regardless of other factors. Lowering the upper age of original juvenile court jurisdiction is often omitted in discussions of juvenile transfer mechanisms, but this method is most likely responsible for the largest number of youths who actually appear in criminal court. As of 1997, 10 States (Georgia, Illinois, Louisiana, Massachusetts, Michigan, Missouri, New Hampshire, South Carolina, Texas, and Wisconsin) excluded all 17-year-olds from their juvenile courts by designating the age of juvenile court jurisdiction as 16 or younger; three States (Connecticut, New York, and North Carolina) excluded all 16-year-olds as well (Griffin, Torbet, and Szymanski 1998, A5–A85).

The number of youths affected by age exclusion laws is likely to be considerable, although no national data on the issue exist. The National Center for Juvenile Justice (NCJJ) estimated that there were 176,000 law violations committed in 1991 by youths under age 18 that were ineligible for juvenile court because State laws excluded 16- and 17-year-olds from the juvenile court (Snyder, Sickmund, and Poe-Yamagata 1995, 155). The NCJJ estimate was produced by applying the 1991 per-capita rate of law violations handled by juvenile courts nationwide (according to *Juvenile Court Statistics*, a Federal reporting series) to the relevant youth populations of each State in which 16- or 17-year-olds were defined as adults for the purposes of criminal prosecution.

The same method can be used to estimate the number of youths excluded from juvenile courts just 5 years later in 1996. According to *Juvenile Court Statistics*, the national rate of law violations handled by juvenile courts in 1996 was 119.8 cases for every 1,000 16-year-olds and 119 cases for every 1,000 17-year-olds in the U.S. population (Stahl 1999). According to the U.S. Census Bureau, there were 380,875 16-year-olds residing in Connecticut, New York, and North Carolina in 1996, and nearly 1.5 million 17-year-olds in these States and the other 10 States that excluded 17-year-olds from juvenile court (see U.S. Bureau of the Census 1999). Using the same method employed by NCJJ for 1991, this analysis suggests that there were as many as 220,000 law violations committed in 1996 by youths younger than 18 who were legally ineligible for juvenile court because of legislative age limits. If only half of these cases actually went forward for criminal court processing, they would still far exceed the number of juveniles ending up in adult court by all other methods combined.

Based on the number of youths affected, it is clear that the actions of State legislators "transferred" far more juveniles to adult court than did either judges or prosecutors. Lowering the upper age of juvenile court jurisdiction allows States to maintain a boundary between juvenile and criminal court while reducing its actual significance. In 1996, more than 40 percent of the delinquency cases handled by juvenile courts nationwide involved youths age 16 or older (Snyder et al. 1998). When States reduce the upper age of juvenile court jurisdiction (as New Hampshire and Wisconsin did in 1996), they likely remove most of their serious and chronic young offenders from juvenile court. This may reduce conflict over the role of the juvenile court in handling serious offenders, but it also eliminates opportunities for the juvenile justice system to intervene aggressively in less serious cases.

Blended sentencing

Transferring juveniles to the adult court system is the most widely recognized method of reducing the significance of the juvenile-criminal border, but it is certainly not the only method. During the last two decades of the 20th century, State lawmakers began to experiment with an array of new policy options for young offenders. For example, some States gave judges the power to "blend" criminal court sentences with juvenile court dispositions (Torbet and Szymanski 1998, 6). Instead of choosing between sentencing a youth in juvenile or adult court, judges can draw on both systems. Blended sentencing policies were devised primarily to provide longer terms of incarceration for juveniles, but they also helped to blur the distinction between juvenile justice and adult justice.

Most States that enacted blended sentencing laws did so by choosing from three basic types of sentencing schemes. The first type of blended sentencing gives either juvenile court judges or criminal court judges the discretion to place youthful offenders with either juvenile or adult correctional agencies, based on the offender's characteristics and the resources of the particular jurisdiction. Florida passed a blended sentencing law that allowed both juvenile and criminal court judges to sentence juveniles to either the juvenile or adult correctional system (Torbet et al. 1996, 14). Judges were required to consider a statutorily defined set of criteria to determine the appropriateness of the two systems. Should the judge determine the juvenile system was the most appropriate for a particular case, the juvenile was found delinquent and sentenced to the juvenile correctional system. If not, the juvenile was found criminally guilty of the offense and sentenced to the adult Department of Corrections. As of 1995, nine States (California, Colorado, Florida, Idaho, Michigan, New Mexico, Oklahoma, Virginia, and West Virginia) had enacted this form of blended sentencing (Torbet et al. 1996).

A second blended sentencing system allows juvenile court judges to impose sentences that sequentially confine offenders to juvenile and adult correctional facilities. Youthful offenders are confined in juvenile facilities until they reach maturity and then transferred into adult correctional facilities to serve the remainder of their sentences. Five States (Colorado, Massachusetts, Rhode Island, South Carolina, and Texas) had adopted this model of blended sentencing by the mid-1990s (Torbet et al. 1996, 13).

A third blended sentencing model allows judges to impose sanctions on youthful offenders in both the juvenile and adult correctional systems simultaneously. Upon completion of the juvenile justice sanction, the adult portion of the sanction is suspended, contingent on the offender's compliance with the particular conditions of disposition. Eight States (Arkansas, Connecticut, Iowa, Kansas, Minnesota, Montana, Missouri, and Virginia) employed this sentencing option as of 1995 (Torbet et al. 1996, 14).

The underlying purpose of all of these sentencing options is to increase the range of punishment available for juvenile offenders regardless of whether the charges are initially processed in the juvenile court or the criminal court. Increasing the variety of sentencing options available may reduce the resistance of court officials to handle very young offenders in the adult system since juveniles are not subject to immediate confinement with adults. They also allow juvenile court judges to draw on the traditionally richer treatment and supervision resources available in the juvenile justice system without having to sacrifice the lengthy periods of incarceration once available only in the criminal court system. Blended sentencing was virtually unheard of in the juvenile justice system until the 1990s. By 1997, there were 20 States employing one or more blended sentencing schemes (Torbet et al. 1996, 13; Torbet and Szymanski 1998, 6) (see exhibit 7).

Mandatory minimum sentences/sentencing guidelines

Sentencing guidelines and mandatory minimum policies for juveniles also began to proliferate during the 1990s. As of 1997, 17 States and the District of Columbia had enacted some type of mandatory minimum sentence provisions for at least some juvenile offenders (Torbet et al. 1996, 14; Torbet and Szymanski 1998, 7–8) (see exhibit 8). Typically, sentencing guidelines applied only in cases involving violent or serious juvenile offenders as defined by statute. Massachusetts adopted a law that required juveniles at least 14 years of age who were found responsible for first-degree murder to serve a sentence of at least 15 years in a correctional facility; juveniles found responsible for second-degree murder were required to serve at least 10 years (Torbet et al. 1996, 15). Some jurisdictions applied sentencing guidelines to young offenders

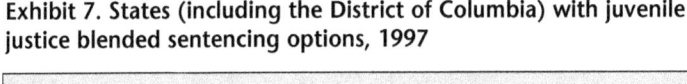

Exhibit 7. States (including the District of Columbia) with juvenile justice blended sentencing options, 1997

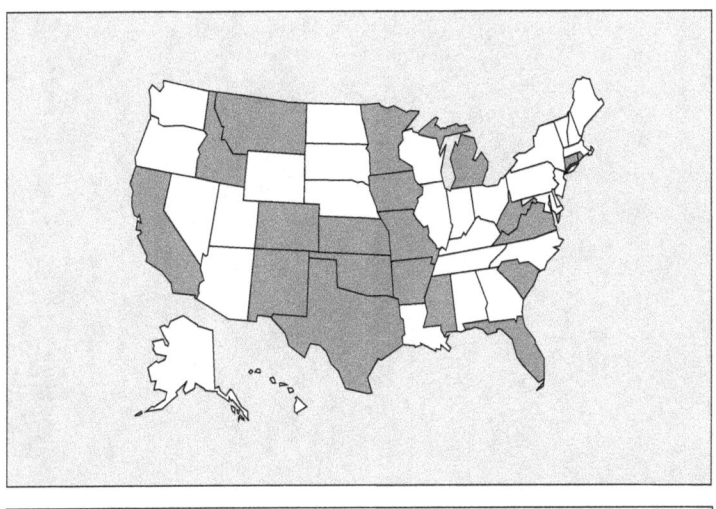

▨ Allowed blended sentencing (20)   ☐ Did not allow blended sentencing (31)

Sources: Torbet et al. 1996, 13; Torbet and Szymanski 1998, 6.

by first requiring that they be tried in criminal court, but others (e.g., Arizona, Utah, and Wyoming) enacted formal sentencing guidelines that applied to juvenile delinquency cases handled by juvenile court judges. These laws required juvenile court dispositions to be consistent with a predefined sentencing menu largely based on the youth's most recent offense and prior record.

Concerns about unstructured, disparate, and even arbitrary sentencing practices for adults have led to the widespread use of sentencing guidelines and mandatory minimum policies in criminal courts during the last three decades of the 20th century (Tonry 1996). States may have started to apply these policies to the juvenile justice system for many of the same reasons. The use of structured sentencing, however, fundamentally contradicts the basic premise of juvenile justice by making sentence length proportional to the severity of an offense rather than basing court outcomes on the characteristics and life problems of an offender. Sentencing guidelines made the juvenile justice process even more similar to criminal justice and thus further diminished the importance of the juvenile-criminal border.

Exhibit 8. States (including the District of Columbia) with sentencing guidelines or mandatory minimum sentences for youths, 1997

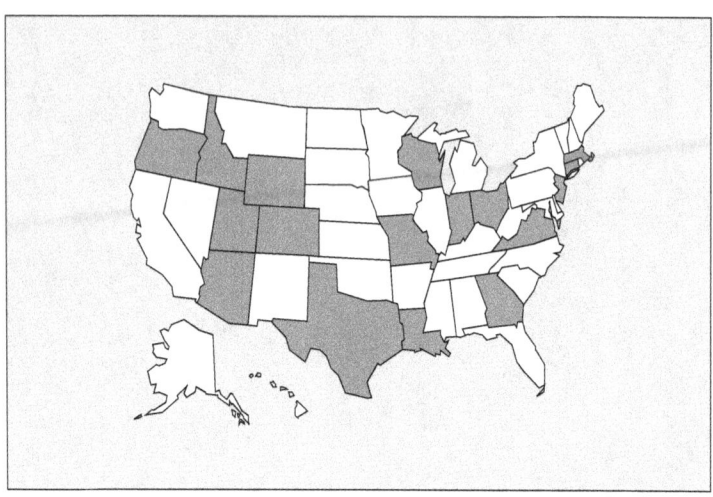

☐ Provided sentencing guidelines (18)   ☐ Did not provide sentencing guidelines (33)

Sources: Torbet et al. 1996, 14; Torbet and Szymanski 1998, 7–8.

Reduced confidentiality

Almost all juvenile court proceedings and records were completely confidential as recently as the 1960s. Confidentiality was an integral part of the traditional juvenile justice model, based on the theory that designating a juvenile as a law violator and then releasing that information to the public would stigmatize a young person in the community. This stigma would then encourage the juvenile to adopt a deviant self-image and reduce any likelihood of rehabilitation within the juvenile justice system (e.g., Schur 1971). As juvenile justice policy became more contentious during the 1980s and 1990s, support for confidentiality protections began to erode. Practical issues such as jurisdictional information sharing and greater media interest in juvenile court proceedings began to win out over confidentiality. Most States began to open their juvenile court proceedings and arrest records to the public and to the media.

By 1997, 30 States had enacted provisions to allow open hearings in at least some juvenile cases (Torbet and Szymanski 1998, 10). Typically, these laws pertained to cases in which a juvenile was alleged to have committed a serious or violent offense or if the juvenile had a certain number of previous juvenile court adjudications. Forty-two States had enacted legislation authorizing the release and publication of the names and addresses of alleged juvenile offenders in at least some cases. Similarly, 48 States allowed the disclosure of juvenile court records to at least one of the following: the public, victims, schools, and/or law enforcement agencies. States also began to allow more juveniles to be finger-printed and photographed for later identification by law enforcement. In fact, only four States did not allow juvenile fingerprints to be included in criminal history records (Maine, New Hampshire, Rhode Island, and Wisconsin), and only five States did not allow juveniles to be photographed (Maine, Nebraska, Rhode Island, West Virginia, and Wisconsin) (Torbet and Szymanski 1998, 10).

Not only have juvenile court documents become less confidential, they have also become more permanent. Traditionally, juvenile court records were sealed after the court's jurisdiction over a youth had expired. These records were often expunged or destroyed after a period of time had passed as long as the juvenile was not convicted of subsequent criminal behavior. Once a juvenile court record was expunged, it was as if the adjudication had never occurred, freeing ex-offenders to deny ever having a police record.

During the 1990s, many States adopted laws that either required juvenile records to remain open longer or prevented the sealing or destruction of juve-nile records altogether, typically those involving violent or serious felonies. Florida required that records regarding juveniles considered habitual offenders must be retained until the offender's 26th birthday (Torbet et al. 1996, 42). North Carolina passed a law preventing authorities from expunging records of juveniles who had committed certain serious offenses (Torbet et al. 1996, 45). By 1997, 25 States had enacted laws restricting the sealing and/or expunging of juvenile records (Torbet and Szymanski 1998, 10).

Use of juvenile records in criminal court

Finally, one of the more significant departures from a traditional system of juvenile justice was the idea that juvenile court records should follow young adults into criminal court. By allowing criminal court judges to consider a defendant's prior juvenile court record at the time of sentencing, States were altering the terms of the agreement that allowed the juvenile court system to exist in the first place. Juvenile law was essentially a covenant between accused juveniles and the State. Young offenders agreed to receive less due process in juvenile court in exchange for a more informal, nonstigmatizing, and nonper-manent disposition. The Supreme Court relied on this covenant when it with-held full legal rights from young people facing juvenile court adjudication.

In 1971, the Supreme Court halted the due process revolution it helped to inspire only 4 years earlier with the *Gault* opinion. The Court ruled in *McKeiver v. Pennsylvania* that juvenile courts were not constitutionally obligated to offer jury trials to accused juvenile offenders (403 U.S. 528 [1971]). The majority opinion in *McKeiver* expressed a fear that imposing juries on the juvenile court might "effectively end the idealistic prospect of an intimate, informal protective proceeding" (p. 545). The Court also maintained that "equating the adjudicative phase of the juvenile proceeding with a criminal trial ignores the aspects of fairness, concern, sympathy, and paternal attention inherent in the juvenile court system" (p. 550). Whether such an atmosphere could be found in actual juvenile courts was debatable even in the 1970s. By the 1990s, however, the emergence of policies that permitted juvenile court records to enhance the severity of criminal court sentences made the issue moot. Defendants could now be imprisoned for many years as a direct result of adjudications in juvenile court.

As of 1997, all 50 States and the District of Columbia had enacted statutes or court rules allowing this practice or they had case law that sanctioned it (Sanborn 1998, 209). Juvenile offense histories were used to enhance criminal court sanctions in at least three ways: as criminal history points in sentencing guideline systems; as aggravating factors considered during sentencing; or as "strikes" in jurisdictions with "three strikes" legislation (Sanborn 1998, 210). Criminal court sentencing guidelines in 13 jurisdictions assigned offenders criminal history points or criminal history categories based on prior juvenile adjudications. Two jurisdictions (North Carolina and Tennessee) allowed prior juvenile adjudications to count as aggravating factors in their guideline systems, and six nonguideline jurisdictions (Alaska, Colorado, Illinois, Indiana, New Jersey, and Ohio) permitted consideration of juvenile adjudications as aggravating factors in at least some cases (Sanborn 1998). For example, Illinois and Indiana allowed juvenile offense histories to serve as sufficient grounds for increasing sentence length or imposing consecutive sentences. Three States (California, Louisiana, and Texas) allowed juvenile adjudications to serve as the first and second strikes against adult offenders. Thus, offenders with two prior juvenile court adjudications could face life in prison if their first appearance in criminal court resulted in conviction for a strike offense.

Research Findings

The broad popularity of sentencing guidelines, blended sentencing, and using juvenile court adjudications to enhance criminal court sentences were all unmistakable signs that State lawmakers were beginning to abandon the traditional concept of juvenile justice. Juvenile justice interventions that once targeted the depth of an offender's troubles were now clearly focused on the gravity of the offender's behavior. Whereas the adequacy of an intervention was once evaluated by its intensity, it would now be judged principally by its duration. By the end of the century, the direction being taken by juvenile justice policy was clear. The States were slowly dismantling the boundary between their juvenile justice and criminal justice systems. Efforts to do away with the boundary seemed to begin almost as soon as the original juvenile courts were founded in the early 20th century, but the Supreme Court's *Gault* decision in 1967 helped accelerate the process.

As lawmakers reinvented the goals and procedures of juvenile courts to make them more like those of criminal courts, they also became increasingly interested in new provisions for transferring some juveniles to adult court. At first, transfer policies focused on a few exceptional cases, such as the most violent offenders and those with lengthy arrest records. Soon, however, transfers were expanded to include drug offenders, juveniles accused of weapon charges, and even many property offenders. States first attempted merely to increase the number of youths waived to criminal court. Later, the procedural difficulties involved in judicial waiver became burdensome and states began to experiment with other methods of exposing more juveniles to the criminal court process, such as legislative exclusion, prosecutor direct file, and blended sentencing.

Why did policymakers turn so instinctively to the criminal court? Most simply assumed that juvenile offenders tried in criminal court would receive more certain and severe punishment. Researchers began to examine this assumption seriously during the 1980s and 1990s. Surprisingly, there were few studies before 1980 that assessed the actual outcomes of criminal court transfer (see reviews in Howell 1997, 88–111; Feld 1998b). Several researchers had examined the decisionmaking processes leading up to transfer, and there was an ample literature about the characteristics of juveniles who were most likely to be transferred. Few researchers, however, had been able to track groups of offenders into the adult system to test whether actual outcomes met the expectations of policymakers.

Targets of transfer

Researchers who analyzed the characteristics of juveniles most likely to be transferred into criminal court generally identified two distinct but overlapping groups (Snyder and Sickmund 1999, 179–182). First, there were the chronic offenders with long histories of arrest and juvenile court involvement. Chronic offenders were especially likely to be transferred as they neared the upper age limit of the juvenile court's jurisdiction. Second, there were the (far fewer) juveniles charged with serious person offenses. Even a single serious offense such as homicide, forcible rape, or armed robbery was usually sufficient to place a youth at high risk of being transferred. Youths in this second group could be virtually any age, especially if the offense involved serious injuries to a victim.

One study sponsored by the Federal juvenile justice office, the Office of Juvenile Justice and Delinquency Prevention (OJJDP), found that waiver requests by Utah prosecutors were nearly always approved (87 percent) in cases where a youth used a weapon to injure a victim (Snyder, Sickmund, and Poe-Yamagata 1999). The same study found that waiver requests were very likely to be approved (81 percent) in cases involving offenders with five or more prior cases in juvenile court. The same researchers found that South Carolina youths with five or more prior arrests were significantly more likely to be waived than juveniles with fewer prior arrests. South Carolina judges approved 82 percent of waiver requests for youths with virtually no offense histories if they were charged with serious violent offenses. Similar findings emerged from other research on transfer (Feld 1999; Howell 1997; U.S. General Accounting Office 1995). Clearly, the probability of criminal court transfer was affected by the length of an offender's law-violating career and the severity of his or her most recent offense.

Court outcomes

As policymakers worked throughout the 1980s and 1990s to expand the pool of juveniles eligible for transfer, researchers began to ask whether criminal court sanctions were in fact more punitive or applied more consistently than those available in juvenile court. The premise that criminal court handling necessarily yielded severe sentences was questioned as early as 1982 by research showing that half of transferred youths received no term of incarceration following a criminal conviction. Hamparian and colleagues (1982) analyzed 1978 data from a multi-State study and found that although the vast majority (91 percent) of juveniles tried in criminal court were convicted, more than half of the convictions resulted in probation, fines, or other nonincarcerative sanctions. Slightly less than half (46 percent) of judicial transfers and 39 percent of prosecutor direct files ended in sentences that involved any term of incarceration (Hamparian et al. 1982).

Another study examined a cohort of 214 youths transferred to criminal court in an unnamed Western State in 1980 and 1981 (Bortner 1986). The results showed that 96 percent of all transferred youths were convicted; 32 percent of the convictions resulted in either jail or prison. Heuser (1984) studied a sample of youths transferred to Oregon criminal courts and found that 81 percent were convicted while 54 percent of the convicted youths were given a term of incarceration. More recently, McNulty (1996) found that 92 percent of transferred cases resulted in convictions, but 43 percent of those transferred received a sentence involving incarceration and 49 percent received probation. Similarly, Fagan (1995, 1996) found that up to 60 percent of transferred youths were found guilty in criminal court but more than half of those convicted received sentences not involving incarceration.

These findings were supported by a study from the Florida Department of Juvenile Justice (Bureau of Data and Research 1999). The agency's analysis of criminal court dispositions for transferred cases showed that only 17 percent of cases sent to adult court actually resulted in admissions to prison and 13 percent resulted in some jail time. Of all transferred cases in Florida (approximately 6,000 per year), the vast majority resulted in either probation (54 percent), acquittal or dismissal (15 percent), or pretrial diversion (1 percent).

Of course, analyzing the rate of incarceration for transferred juveniles does not fully address the concerns of policymakers. The underlying question is, "Compared with what?" Even if criminal court transfer cannot guarantee a serious sentence, does it at least improve the odds of one? Also, does criminal court handling increase the chances that a youthful offender will receive a more lengthy term of incarceration? A few studies have examined these issues by comparing youths retained in juvenile court with youths transferred to criminal court. The results generally indicate that young offenders convicted of violent crimes in criminal court receive sanctions that are more punitive, while nonviolent youths receive similar (or even lighter) sentences than they would likely have received in juvenile court.

In a particularly effective study, Fagan (1995, 1996) compared a sample of youths retained in northern New Jersey's juvenile court system with a sample of youths excluded from southeastern New York's juvenile court system. Both samples were composed of offenders age 15 or 16, charged with a burglary or robbery offense in 1981–82. In New York, the youths were prosecuted in criminal court because they were already statutorily excluded from juvenile court. In New Jersey, offenders of the same age and charged with similar offenses were usually handled in juvenile court. The samples were selected at random from two New Jersey counties and two New York counties and then matched on a number of legal and social measures. Researchers followed each sample for 4 years.

The results of the Fagan study suggested that offenders charged with robbery may have been punished more often and incarcerated more often in criminal court, but burglary offenders were punished similarly in either court (Fagan 1995, 248). Robbery offenders in criminal court were found guilty more often (57 percent) than their matched counterparts in juvenile court (46 percent). Likewise, among offenders found guilty of robbery, those handled in criminal court were significantly more likely to be incarcerated (46 percent) than were cases processed in juvenile court (18 percent). In contrast, offenders charged with burglary in criminal court were no more likely to be convicted or incarcerated than the matched sample of youths charged in juvenile courts. Moreover, for offenders incarcerated for either robbery or burglary, the duration of incarceration was not significantly different by court type. Both types of offenders received indeterminate sentences with a range of approximately 11 to 32 months (Fagan 1995, 249).

Podkopacz and Feld (1996) used data from Minnesota to compare dispositions for youths in juvenile court and criminal court. The results suggested that youths convicted in criminal court were much more likely to be sentenced to confinement (85 percent) than were youths handled in juvenile court (63 percent), even after controlling for the seriousness of offenses. Youths convicted of offenses carrying presumptive terms of incarceration (e.g., violent offenses), received much longer sentences from the criminal court (roughly 4 years) than from the juvenile court (approximately 9 months). The relationship reversed, however, for youths convicted of nonpresumptive offenses (usually property). Youths adjudicated for these offenses in juvenile court were sentenced to longer periods of incarceration (about 6 months) than were youths convicted in criminal court (about 4.5 months).

Together, studies of transfer outcomes suggest that conviction rates for transferred youths may vary from 60 to 90 percent, with 30 to 60 percent of convictions resulting in at least some incarceration. In other words, the odds of incarceration might vary from a low of 2 to a high of 5 or 6 incarcerations for every 10 transfers. The most recent research suggests that the odds of incarceration for transferred youths are contingent on the offenses involved in each case. Youths convicted of violent offenses are more likely to be incarcerated if they are handled in criminal court. Youths charged with property and drug offenses, on the other hand, tend to receive sentences in criminal court that are no more (and sometimes less) severe than the dispositions usually imposed by juvenile court.

Youth outcomes

Court sanctions, of course, are a means to an end. Policymakers who advocate transfer argue that greater use of the adult court will provide more severe sanctions and thus a more effective deterrent to crime, either among youths actually transferred (specific deterrence) or among other potential offenders (general deterrence). Either effect is difficult to measure, and the few studies that have tried to do so have generally found little to no effect from criminal court transfer. In a study of the specific deterrent effects of transfer, for example, Fagan (1995) found that youths convicted of robbery in adult court reoffended more quickly and more frequently than those adjudicated in juvenile court. Most of the youths in both robbery groups reoffended during the followup period, but time until rearrest for robbery offenders sentenced in juvenile court was 50 percent longer than for robbery offenders sentenced in criminal court. Approximately 81 percent of burglars in both courts were rearrested during the study, and no significant differences were found in time to rearrest when burglars adjudicated in juvenile court were compared with those convicted in adult court.

Another often-cited study analyzed matched samples of youths in Florida and found similar results (Bishop et al. 1996; Winner et al. 1997). The study matched retained and transferred youths on seven criteria: most serious offense, number of counts in current case, number of prior referrals to juvenile court, most serious prior offense, age, gender, and race. All youths in the study entered the justice system during 1987, and their subsequent offending was followed through 1994. The Florida researchers concluded that criminal court transfer was "more likely to aggravate recidivism than to stem it" (Winner et al. 1997, 558–559). Half of the youths in both samples were rearrested and multivariate analyses revealed that transferred and retained youths had similar patterns of reoffending, although some property offenders convicted in criminal court had a lower rate of rearrest than their counterparts retained in juvenile court. Transferred youths generally reoffended more quickly than did youths retained in the juvenile justice system, but the prevalence of recidivism for retained youths eventually caught up to the level of transferred youths. Among the youths who recidivated, transferred youths tended to reoffend more often and more quickly. Other analyses have found similar results. For example, Podkopacz and Feld (1996) found that transferred youths in Minnesota were more likely than nontransferred youths to reoffend (58 percent versus 42 percent over 24 months at large).

If expanded criminal court transfer policies do increase public safety, researchers have yet to find clear evidence of that effect. Some studies find that transfer increases the certainty and severity of sanctions for the most serious and violent youths sent to criminal court, but these cases represent about one-third of transferred juveniles. In most nonviolent cases young offenders receive sentences comparable to what they might have received from a juvenile court.

Researchers investigating the general deterrent effect of juvenile transfer laws failed to find clear associations between transfer and public safety. Singer (1996) as well as Singer and McDowall (1988) examined the impact of New York State laws that automatically transferred any juvenile from ages 13 to 15 who committed one of several violent offenses (murder, robbery, serious assaults, etc.). The law required such juveniles to serve relatively long sentences in secure facilities. (Recall that New York already handled all youths 16 and older in criminal court.) Under the new policy, juveniles as young as age 13 who were convicted of second-degree murder were mandated to a sentence of not less than 5 years in a secure facility. Offenders age 14 and older and convicted of various other violent offenses were required to serve similarly long mandatory minimum sentences.

To evaluate the general deterrent effect of the new law, Singer used interrupted time series and regression models to compare monthly arrest rates for youths affected by the law with two groups of youths not affected. Philadelphia juveniles comprised the first comparison group. For the second group, Singer chose New York youths ages 16 to 18 and thus not eligible for juvenile court. The analysis suggested the new law had no consistent or significant effects on juvenile violence. In most instances where arrest rates appeared to fall after enactment of the policy, the effect was not consistent across the State of New York. Rates may have dropped for some offenses in upstate New York but not in New York City (or vice versa), raising doubts about the influence of the statewide policy. Where arrest rates did drop in New York City, there were usually comparable declines in Philadelphia, where transfer laws had not changed substantially. According to Singer, the results indicated that "a switch in legal setting and an increase in the severity of punishment does not necessarily lead to a reduction in violent juvenile crime" (Singer 1996, 164).

A study in Georgia also failed to detect a significant difference in the rate of juvenile offending following enactment of expanded transfer provisions, suggesting that the broader use of criminal court transfer did not have a general deterrent effect (Risler, Sweatman, and Nackerud 1998). The same conclusion was reached by Jensen and Metsger (1994) who compared changes in juvenile violence in Idaho, which had recently expanded its transfer laws, to crime in Montana, which had not changed its laws. The analysis failed to find a significant difference in rates of violence following the implementation of Idaho's broader transfer provisions.

The bottom line on transfer effects

The consensus appears to be that increasing the use of criminal court for young offenders does not ensure conviction for youths handled in adult court and does not guarantee incarceration even for those youths who are convicted. If expanded criminal court transfer policies do increase public safety, researchers have yet to find clear evidence of that effect. Some studies find that transfer increases the certainty and severity of sanctions for the most serious and violent youths sent to criminal court, but these cases represent about one-third of transferred juveniles. In most nonviolent cases (perhaps half of transferred youths), young offenders receive sentences comparable to what they might have received from a juvenile court. Some juveniles (about one-fifth of transferred cases) actually get more lenient treatment in criminal court because they are convicted of lesser offenses or the charges against them are dismissed.

Critics of the available research on transfer point out that many studies are not well designed and fail to account for all of the factors that go into actual transfer decisions (Snyder and Sickmund 1999, 182). These criticisms have merit in some cases. Research that compares one group of youths chosen for transfer with another group of youths retained in juvenile court is undoubtedly affected by selection bias. Judges and prosecutors who elect to transfer certain juveniles to criminal court must base their decisions on some criteria of dangerousness and/or amenability, even if those criteria are unmeasured impressions or gut instincts. Youths transferred to criminal court, therefore, may be systematically different from youths retained in juvenile court, despite researchers' efforts to match transferred and nontransferred samples using objective criteria.

The "selection bias" argument, however, cannot explain why youths who are statutorily defined as adults in one jurisdiction are no less likely to recidivate than youths defined as juveniles in another jurisdiction. The Fagan (1995, 1996) study compared youths handled in the criminal courts of New York with similar youths handled by New Jersey juvenile courts. There were no case-specific decisions by judges or prosecutors. The two groups were handled differently as a matter of State law. Similarly, selection bias cannot explain the finding that transfer policies have no measurable effect on general deterrence or on aggregate arrest rates.

One explanation for the inability of researchers to document the effects of criminal court transfer may be that policies designed to expand the use of transfer are never implemented exactly as legislators hope they will be. A number of researchers have pointed out that the justice system is a complex network of individual decisions, and the network often responds in ways not anticipated by reform-minded legislators (Emerson 1991; Singer 1996; Zimring 1991). For example, Singer (1996, 97–151) provides a convincing case that the juvenile justice system is "loosely coupled." There are so many centers of discretion in the juvenile justice system that the decisions of any individual or group are at best an imperfect reflection of the decisions and priorities of others. Police do not refer every arrested youth for prosecution. Prosecutors do not charge every young offender referred by police. Judges do not adjudicate every offender charged by prosecutors. According to Singer, loose coupling creates a justice system in

> *As a crime control policy, criminal court transfer may symbolize toughness more than it actually delivers toughness. Moreover, the symbol may have a high price.*

which individual case processing decisions are structured by interorganizational negotiations, thus reducing the chances that a single policy initiative will have a consistent effect on crime. Ironically, loose coupling also tends to increase the system's need for potent symbols of uniformity such as criminal court transfer.

Singer's organizational explanation for the relative ineffectiveness of criminal court transfer was supported by the findings of a 1999 study funded by OJJDP (Snyder and Sickmund 1999). Researchers in Pennsylvania studied nearly 500 court cases that were automatically excluded from that State's juvenile courts by a 1996 law that transferred youths age 15 and older if they were charged with certain violent offenses (robbery, aggravated assault, etc.) and had either committed the offense with a weapon or were previously adjudicated for an excluded crime. Prior to 1996, Pennsylvania had relied largely on judicial waivers to send serious juvenile offenders to criminal court. The new law automatically transferred many juveniles who were routinely waived by judges, but it also targeted youths who would have been unlikely candidates for waiver (i.e., very young offenders, females, and those with limited arrest records). Researchers used data from three counties to track court outcomes for 473 juveniles that met the new criteria for automatic exclusion from juvenile court. Each case was followed through several stages of prosecution and trial.

In half of the cases targeted for exclusion, criminal courts either declined to prosecute or sent the youth back to juvenile court using "de-certification" procedures (Snyder and Sickmund 1999, 180). Nearly one-fifth (19 percent) of the excluded cases were dismissed during preliminary hearings; 31 percent were returned to juvenile court. Even when cases were approved for criminal prosecution, more than half ended in dismissal, probation, or other sentences not involving incarceration. The youths least likely to be convicted and incarcerated by criminal courts were similar to the youths who were least likely to have been waived under the pre-1996 judicial waiver system. They tended to be younger, less likely to use weapons, and less likely to have an extensive prior offense history. Thus, in the end, Pennsylvania's new law appeared to achieve little.

Like many of their counterparts across the United States, Pennsylvania lawmakers sought to expand the use of adult court for young offenders, but their method of accomplishing that goal swept many younger and less serious offenders into criminal court. The system adapted to the policy by dismissing more cases prior to trial, sending more youths back to juvenile court, and imposing community-based sentences on many of the remaining youths. In terms of public safety, the results were comparable. The transferred youths who actually ended up in jail or prison were basically the same type of youths who were traditionally waived to criminal court prior to 1996. Before the new law came into effect, juvenile court judges waived fewer cases, but in most of the cases they waived (77 percent), the youths were incarcerated (Snyder and Sickmund 1999, 181). Of all the youths who were automatically excluded by the new law, only 19 percent were incarcerated following criminal court convictions.

Juvenile probation officers, prosecutors, and judges openly embrace the goals of retribution and incapacitation, just as in the adult system. Policymakers, the media, and many juvenile justice professionals sometimes do not even bother with the euphemisms of juvenile justice. Delinquency offenses are simply called crimes. Trial is an easy synonym for an adjudication hearing.

As a crime control policy, criminal court transfer may symbolize toughness more than it actually delivers toughness. Moreover, the symbol may have a high price. Sending more juveniles to adult court may not result in significantly more punishment for more offenders, but it may mean longer pretrial delays, more pretrial incarceration with few services to address youth problems, greater population management problems in prisons and jails, and greater exposure of youths to adult inmates (Howell 1997, 109; Snyder and Sickmund 1999, 180). Fagan (1996, 100–101) concluded as much after reviewing long-term outcomes for youths tried as adults with those retained in juvenile court:

> By neither public safety nor punishment (or just deserts) standards can claims be made that the criminal justice system affords greater accountability for adolescent felony offenders or protection for the public. If criminalization is intended to instill accountability, its effects are diluted by the lengthier case processing time. If it is intended to protect the public by making incarceration more certain and terms lengthier, it fails also on this count. While these processes may have symbolic value to the public, they seem to offer little substantive advantage in the legal response to adolescent crimes. It is only for the earlier accumulation of a criminal record, leading to lengthier terms and more severe punishments for subsequent offenses, that there is a marginal gain in the relocation of adolescent crimes to the criminal court.

The increasing use of the criminal court for young offenders may have also contributed to the perception that juvenile justice is somehow deficient and that any serious attempt to control crime must involve a criminal trial. In combination with other policy changes, such as reduced confidentiality, sentencing guidelines, and policies that use juvenile adjudications to enhance criminal sentences, the increased use of transfer during the 1980s and 1990s may have helped to facilitate the erosion of legal and procedural barriers that once separated juvenile justice and criminal justice.

Juvenile Justice in the 21st Century

There can be little remaining doubt that the boundary between juvenile justice and criminal justice has become less meaningful than originally envisioned by the founders of the juvenile court. All 50 States and the District of Columbia continue to operate separate juvenile courts, but many youths are ineligible for juvenile court and those that remain experience a juvenile court process that is far more criminalized (Feld 1993). Juvenile court procedures are more complex and evidence driven; delinquency cases are more likely to be formally charged by prosecutors instead of being handled informally by juvenile probation workers (Butts 1997a; Shine and Price 1992). Juvenile court dispositions are increasingly governed by offense severity rather than by youth troubles (Bazemore and Umbreit 1995; Feld 1998a). Defense attorneys are expected to defend juvenile clients more vigorously since adjudication may lead to severe sanctions (Puritz et al. 1995; Sanborn 1998). Juvenile probation officers, prosecutors, and judges openly embrace the goals of retribution and incapacitation, just as in the adult system. Policymakers, the media, and many juvenile justice professionals sometimes do not even bother with the euphemisms of juvenile justice. Delinquency offenses are simply called crimes. Trial is an easy synonym for an adjudication hearing. Secure facilities are often called youth prisons. In short, the similarities of the juvenile and adult justice systems are becoming greater than the differences between them.

Some elements of the juvenile-criminal border, however, remain in place. Constitutional protections for juveniles failed to keep up with the criminalization of juvenile justice. The underlying premise of the juvenile justice system has always been that youths accused of delinquency need fewer due process rights because the juvenile court is designed to help rather than punish. Most of the legislative and policy initiatives that increased the punishment orientation of juvenile courts occurred during the 1980s and 1990s. Yet the last significant enhancements to the constitutional rights of juveniles occurred during the 1960s and 1970s. In the majority of States, juveniles still have no right to jury trial, no guarantee of bail consideration, and no right to a speedy trial (Butts and Sanborn 1999; Sanborn 1993).

Efforts to rework the juvenile justice system are unlikely to diminish in the coming decades. In March 2000, 62 percent of California voters endorsed sweeping changes in the State's juvenile justice system by passing Proposition 21, the Gang Violence and Juvenile Crime Prevention Act. The law reduced confidentiality in the juvenile court, limited the use of probation for young offenders, and increased the power of prosecutors to send juveniles to adult court and put them in adult prisons. Public support for the measure was undiminished by projections that it would increase operational costs in the California juvenile justice system by $500 million annually (Nieves 2000). National political leaders call for additional reforms and openly chastise the juvenile court. One U.S. Senator described the juvenile justice system as "ancient, archaic, and broken down" (Domenici 1997, S5898). Another Senator admitted that he could see why "State legislatures around this country are proposing bills to get rid of the juvenile justice system altogether" (Wyden 1997, S2341). The issue is no longer *whether* the boundary between juvenile and criminal justice should be changed, but how much and how fast it should be changed.

What next?

The crux of the debate is how the legal system should respond to crime by young people, and whether that response requires a completely separate court, with noncriminal jurisdiction that is not governed by criminal procedure. This debate tends to polarize around two extremes. One extreme says that the reforms of the 1980s and 1990s were ill-conceived. This position suggests that the traditional juvenile court should be fully restored, including its expanded powers of intervention, lessened due process burden, and a greater emphasis on prevention and rehabilitation. The other extreme holds that the juvenile court ideal never existed in reality and that juvenile courts never offered more than a *mirage* of treatment within a constitutionally defective process. According to this view, juvenile courts should simply be abolished.

Policymakers may need to devise a "third way," a new system of youth justice that does not rely on an all-or-nothing, juvenile-versus-adult dichotomy.

As each policy reform from the 1980s and 1990s added to the punitive power of juvenile courts, the arguments of the abolitionists (best represented by Feld 1998a) became harder to avoid. The research basis for a separate juvenile court was significantly undermined by the criminalization of juvenile justice (see exhibit 9), and the growing similarity of juvenile and criminal justice makes the constitutional bargain that gave birth to the juvenile court increasingly untenable. It was already becoming difficult to believe in the traditional

Exhibit 9. Implications of research for the continued existence of separate courts for adolescent offenders

Reasons for keeping the juvenile court separate	Consensus of research evidence	Verdict for juvenile court
Children and adolescents do not possess adult powers of reason and are not fully responsible for their behavior.	Children begin to exhibit adultlike reason several years before the upper age of juvenile court jurisdiction. A juvenile court based on this premise alone would most likely extend only through ages 12 or 13.	Abolish
The criminal behavior of young offenders is less serious than that of adults.	Offenders generally do not escalate the severity of their criminal behavior with age. Adult courts also handle a wide range of behaviors, including large numbers of minor crimes.	Abolish
Young people are more malleable than adults and respond better to intervention.	Individual differences in treatment amenability emerge between ages 8 and 10 and do not appear to change substantially after age 10.	Abolish
Separate courts help maintain support for separate correctional facilities. Young offenders are isolated from corrupting and possibly predatory older inmates.	Separate correctional facilities for young offenders are possible regardless of which court imposes sentence. Research has *not* found adult facilities to be significantly more crime inducing than juvenile facilities, but juveniles have a higher risk of victimization if incarcerated with adult inmates.	Possibly retain
Separate juvenile courts help reserve a share of treatment and supervision resources specifically for young offenders.	The same argument could apply to other groups of offenders. By itself, this is inadequate justification for a separate legal jurisdiction for young offenders.	Abolish
Juvenile courts prevent the stigma of criminal conviction, thus preserving the life chances of youths who can stay out of further trouble after one or two early mistakes.	As long as juvenile court is less stigmatizing, this is a clear benefit of separate courts. Of course, the same argument could apply to adult defendants who remain crime free for several years.	Retain

Source: Based in part on Hirschi and Gottfredson 1993, 262–271.

juvenile court in 1971 when the Supreme Court denied juveniles the right to jury trial by lauding the "fairness, concern, sympathy, and paternal attention inherent in the juvenile court system" (*McKeiver* v. *Pennsylvania*, 403 U.S. 528, 550 [1971]). By the end of the 20th century, it was impossible to recognize most juvenile courts in the Court's description.

> *Courts that are asked to handle cases involving 13-year-old sex offenders and 14-year-old drug dealers require innovative methods at the charging, investigation, and factfinding stages of the court process, not only at disposition and sentencing.*

State and Federal policymakers who found themselves trapped between two extremes tried to fashion a middle ground. They maintained the juvenile court as an institution while transforming its mission and methods. Unfortunately, this approach created a system that critics say protects neither the public safety nor youth rights. The juvenile justice system may be tougher, but juvenile courts in turn are more attentive to detail and more cautious in deciding adjudications. The entire process moves more deliberately and less creatively. Decades of reform may have increased the severity of the juvenile court process for some offenders, but they reduced the juvenile court's ability to provide individualized and comprehensive interventions for the majority of young offenders.

Conflicts over the juvenile-criminal border have become a corrosive distraction for policymakers, practitioners, and the public. Public safety proponents are unduly focused on increasing the use of criminal court transfer, regardless of the actual effects of transfer. Youth advocates have painted themselves into a corner, forced to concede ever-larger portions of the juvenile court caseload to criminal courts in order to retain discretion over the youthful offenders who remain. Meanwhile, growing numbers of youths as young as 14 years of age are being tried and sentenced in criminal courts that are often not prepared to create specialized procedures and programs to address the problems of developing adolescents. Practitioners find it difficult to create innovative solutions because they are caught up in the struggle over who controls the juvenile-criminal boundary.

Youth justice and alternative court dockets

Policymakers may need to devise a "third way," a new system of youth justice that does not rely on an all-or-nothing, juvenile-versus-adult dichotomy. Some advocates of juvenile court abolition have recommended that policymakers consider an "integrated" criminal system in which youthfulness is included as a mitigating factor in the sentencing phase of criminal trials (Feld 1998a). This approach, however, seems to fall short as an alternative process. Courts that are asked to handle cases involving 13-year-old sex offenders and 14-year-old drug dealers require innovative methods at the charging, investigation, and factfinding stages of the court process, not only at disposition and sentencing.

Other critics of the current system have proposed that courts need more boundaries rather than fewer. Springer (1991, 413) suggests that the current delinquency jurisdiction could be divided into two branches, one for "real children" and another for adolescents older than age 14 or 15. The children's branch could operate as the juvenile court was originally designed, with fewer procedural formalities and a mission of prevention and rehabilitation. The branch for older offenders would operate more like a criminal court and be free to impose harsh dispositions for purely retributive purposes. This plan may solve some problems, but it would encourage policymakers to continue to be distracted by transfers across boundaries rather than focusing their energies on creating a single, more effective process for all offenders.

Others observers have proposed a different approach that essentially combines Feld's abolitionist ideals with the more practical divide-and-conquer strategy of Springer. Butts and Harrell (1998) suggest that policymakers consider an integrated court structure that would no longer depend on the politically untenable premise that acts of "delinquency" are different from "crimes." Designing an integrated court structure, however, would require more than simply moving all youths into the existing criminal court process. An integrated process would have to recognize that adolescents are not adults, that the factors bringing youths to court require special consideration, and that the entire court process should involve an individualized, problem-solving approach rather than simply fact finding and sentencing.

One way to begin designing such an integrated court structure could be to draw on the innovations emerging from drug courts and other specialized courts, including gun courts and domestic violence courts. During the 1990s, criminal court systems around the country began experimenting with specialized dockets to promote more effective criminal justice interventions. Specialized courts were not intended to replace the criminal court, but they offer what in many cases may be a more effective strategy than the traditional criminal court for reducing crime among selected types of offenders. Many alternative courts have incorporated the following values and case-handling methods that are similar to those developed by the original juvenile courts (Butts and Harrell 1998):

■ Treatment and rehabilitation programs are individually matched to offender characteristics.

■ Judges personally supervise treatment agreements with offenders and monitor their compliance.

■ The court uses a combination of immediate penalties and rewards that are contingent on offender behavior.

■ The entire process relies heavily on community-based programs for delivering services and sanctions.

After 30 years, the direction of juvenile justice policy appears unlikely to reverse. Eventually, the justice system may need to adapt to a new environment in which all criminal matters are referred to a single system, regardless of the offender's age.

A coordinated set of specialized dockets for young offenders could offer an effective means of responding to the wide variety of cases now seen in juvenile court, but without the politically provocative all-or-nothing boundary between juvenile and criminal justice. Instead of focusing on a single transfer decision, prosecutors, judges and policymakers could channel youthful offenders into a range of courts, each of which is designed to provide a different combination of treatment, supervision, restorative justice, and public safety. Policymakers could use this new array of courts to build an integrated youth justice system rather than continue battling over the forced choice of juvenile versus criminal jurisdiction.

Conclusion

At the close of the 20th century, policymakers throughout the United States have greatly dissolved the border between juvenile and criminal justice. Young people who violate the law are no longer guaranteed special consideration from the legal system. Some form of juvenile court still exists in every State, but the purposes and procedures of juvenile courts are becoming indistinguishable from those of criminal courts. After 30 years, the direction of juvenile justice policy appears unlikely to reverse. Eventually, the justice system may need to adapt to a new environment in which all criminal matters are referred to a single system, regardless of the offender's age. Of course, children and adolescents will always be cognitively, emotionally, and socially different from adults. Abolishing the legal boundary between juvenile and criminal court does not eliminate all the challenges faced by courts in responding to youth crime. As criminal courts begin to handle even more of the 14- and 15-year-olds who were once the responsibility of juvenile courts, judges and prosecutors will need to devise special procedures and programs for youths. Trial procedures for adolescents may need to be more attuned to the social environment of young offenders. Youths may require specially designed pretrial investigations, speedier case movement, and a wider array of sentencing options. A new youth justice system will have to be devised that can handle all types of young offenders promptly and effectively, even if the legal distinction between crime and delinquency no longer applies. Considerable work will be necessary to design and implement such a system. Unfortunately, this work is being neglected while researchers, practitioners, and elected officials continue to focus on the implications of transfers across a boundary that is rapidly becoming less meaningful.

The authors are grateful to the Urban Institute's State Policy Center and its director, Blaine Liner, for partially funding the preparation of this chapter. Support and assistance was provided by Adele Harrell, director of the Program on Law & Behavior within the State Policy Center, and by Janeen Buck, research associate in the Program on Law & Behavior. Valuable comments and criticisms were also provided by the editorial board of this volume and by Patricia Torbet of the National Center for Juvenile Justice.

Note

1. We use the term "juvenile justice" to refer to the policies and activities of law enforcement and the courts in handling law violations by youths under the age of criminal jurisdiction (usually age 17 and younger). We use the term "juvenile justice system" to refer to these agencies as well as to the other agencies that respond to juvenile offenders once the court process is completed (probation, corrections, etc.). This discussion of the juvenile court refers only to its responsibilities for young offenders and does not apply to the court's involvement in other matters involving children and youths (status offenses, abuse and neglect, child custody matters, etc.).

References

Bazemore, Gordon, and Mark Umbreit. 1995. Rethinking the sanctioning function in juvenile court: Retributive or restorative responses to youth crime. *Crime & Delinquency* 41 (3): 296–316.

Beemsterboer, Mathew J. 1960. The juvenile court—Benevolence in the star chamber. *Journal of Criminal Law, Criminology, and Police Science* 50:464. Quoted in Christopher P. Manfredi, *The Supreme Court and juvenile justice* (Lawrence: University Press of Kansas, 1998), 39.

Bernard, Thomas J. 1992. *The cycle of juvenile justice.* New York: Oxford University Press.

Bishop, Donna M., Charles E. Frazier, Lonn Lanza-Kaduce, and Lawrence Winner. 1996. The transfer of juveniles to criminal court: Does it make a difference? *Crime & Delinquency* 42:171–191.

Bortner, M.A. 1986. Traditional rhetoric, organization realities: Remand of juveniles to adult court. *Crime & Delinquency* 32:53–73.

Bureau of Data and Research. 1999. Dispositions of cases transferred to adult court: Report of the Classification Work Group, Florida Department of Juvenile Justice. Retrieved 17 March 2000 from the World Wide Web: http://www.djj.state.fl.us/RnD/presentations/ClassificationOct99.htm.

Butts, Jeffrey A. 1997a. Juvenile court processing of delinquency cases, 1985–1994. OJJDP Fact Sheet, FS–9757. Washington, D.C.: U.S. Department of Justice, Office of Juvenile Justice and Delinquency Prevention.

———. 1997b. The National Juvenile Court Data Archive: Collecting data since 1927. OJJDP Fact Sheet, FS–9766. Washington, D.C.: U.S. Department of Justice, Office of Juvenile Justice and Delinquency Prevention.

Butts, Jeffrey A., and Adele V. Harrell. 1998. Delinquents or criminals: Policy options for young offenders. Crime Policy Report. Washington, D.C.: Urban Institute.

Butts, Jeffrey A., and Joseph B. Sanborn, Jr. 1999. Is juvenile justice just too slow? *Judicature* 83:16–24.

Clarke, Elizabeth E. 1996. A case for reinventing juvenile transfer: The record of transfer of juvenile offenders to criminal court in Cook County, Illinois. *Juvenile and Family Court Journal* 47:3–21.

Domenici, Peter. 1997. Senator Domenici of New Mexico, floor speech. S. 10, 105th Cong., 1st sess. *Congressional Record*, 18 June, vol. 143, no. 85.

Emerson, Robert M. 1991. Case processing and interorganizational knowledge: Detecting the "real reasons" for referrals. *Social Problems* 38:198–211.

Fagan, Jeffrey. 1996. The comparative advantage of juvenile versus criminal court sanctions on recidivism among adolescent felony offenders. *Law & Policy* 18:77–113.

———. 1995. Separating the men from the boys: The comparative advantage of juvenile versus criminal court sanctions on recidivism among adolescent felony offenders. In *Sourcebook on serious, violent, and chronic juvenile offenders*, edited by James C. Howell, Barry Krisberg, J. David Hawkins, and John J. Wilson. Thousand Oaks, California: Sage Publications.

Feld, Barry C. 1999. Bad kids—Race and the transformation of the juvenile court. New York: Oxford University Press.

———. 1998a. Abolish the juvenile court: Youthfulness, criminal responsibility, and sentencing policy. *Journal of Criminal Law and Criminology* 88:68–136.

———. 1998b. Juvenile and criminal justice systems' responses. In *Youth violence*, edited by M. Tonry and M. Moore. Vol. 24 of *Crime and justice: A review of research*. Chicago: University of Chicago Press.

———. 1993. Criminalizing the American juvenile court. In *Crime and justice: A review of research*, edited by M. Tonry. Vol. 17. Chicago: University of Chicago Press.

———. 1987. The juvenile court meets the principle of the offense: Legislative changes in juvenile waiver statutes. *Journal of Criminal Law and Criminology* 78:471–533.

Fox, Sanford J. 1970. Juvenile justice reform: An historical perspective. *Stanford Law Review* 22:1187–1239.

Griffin, Patrick, Patricia Torbet, and Linda Szymanski. 1998. *Trying juveniles as adults in criminal court: An analysis of State transfer provisions*. OJJDP Report, NCJ 172836. Washington, D.C.: U.S. Department of Justice, Office of Juvenile Justice and Delinquency Prevention.

Hamparian, Donna M., L. Estep, S. Muntean, R. Prestino, R. Swisher, P. Wallace, and J.L. White. 1982. *Youth in adult courts: Between two worlds*. Major Issues in Juvenile Justice Training and Information, NCJ 80823. Washington D.C.: U.S. Department of Justice, Office of Juvenile Justice and Delinquency Prevention.

Heuser, James Paul. 1984. *A statistical study of juveniles arrested for serious felony crime in Oregon and "remanded" to adult criminal court*. Salem: Oregon Department of Justice, Crime Analysis Center.

Hirschi, Travis, and Michael Gottfredson. 1993. Rethinking the juvenile justice system. *Crime & Delinquency* 39:262–271.

Howell, James C. 1997. *Juvenile justice and youth violence*. Thousand Oaks, California: Sage Publications.

Hutzler, J. 1982. Canon to the left, canon to the right: Can the juvenile court survive? *Today's Delinquent* 1. Referenced in Patricia Torbet, Richard Gable, Hunter Hurst IV, Imogene Montgomery, Linda Szymanski, and Douglas Thomas, *State responses to serious and violent juvenile crime*, Research Report, NCJ 161565 (Washington, D.C.: U.S. Department of Justice, Office of Juvenile Justice and Delinquency Prevention, 1996), 4.

Jensen, Eric L., and Linda K. Metsger. 1994. A test of the deterrent effect of legislative waiver on violent juvenile crime. *Crime & Delinquency* 40:96–104.

Leeper, June L. 1991. Recent issues in juvenile jurisdictional waiver hearings. *Journal of Juvenile Law* 12:35–46.

Mack, Julian. 1909. The juvenile court. *Harvard Law Review* 23 (104): 119–120.

Manfredi, Christopher P. 1998. *The Supreme Court and juvenile justice*. Lawrence: University Press of Kansas.

McNulty, Elizabeth W. 1996. The transfer of juvenile offenders to adult court: Panacea or problem? *Law & Policy* 18:61–75.

Mennel, Robert M. 1973. *Thorns and thistles: Juvenile delinquents in the United States 1825–1940.* Hanover, New Hampshire: University Press of New England.

Nieves, Evelyn. 2000. The 2000 campaign: California; Those opposed to 2 initiatives had little chance from start. *New York Times,* 9 March, national ed.

Paulsen, Monrad. 1957. Fairness to the juvenile offender. *Minnesota Law Review* 41:547, 569. Quoted in Christopher P. Manfredi, *The Supreme Court and juvenile justice* (Lawrence: University Press of Kansas, 1998), 38.

Platt, Anthony M. 1977. *The child savers: The invention of delinquency.* Chicago: University of Chicago Press.

Podkopacz, Marcy R., and Barry C. Feld. 1996. The end of the line: An empirical study of judicial waiver. *Journal of Criminal Law and Criminology* 86:449–492.

Polier, Justine Wise. 1989. *Juvenile justice in double jeopardy: The distanced community and vengeful retribution.* Mahwah, New Jersey: Lawrence Erlbaum Associates.

Poulos, Tammy Meredith, and Stan Orchowsky. 1994. Serious juvenile offenders: Predicting the probability of transfer of criminal court. *Crime & Delinquency* 40:3–17.

Puritz, Patricia, Sue Burrell, Robert Schwartz, Mark Soler, and Loren Warboys. 1995. *A call for justice: An assessment of access to counsel and quality of representation in delinquency proceedings.* Washington, D.C.: American Bar Association, in collaboration with the Youth Law Center, the Juvenile Law Center, and the U.S. Department of Justice, Office of Juvenile Justice and Delinquency Prevention.

Risler, Edwin A., Tim Sweatman, and Larry Nackerud. 1998. Evaluating the Georgia legislative waiver's effectiveness in deterring juvenile crime. *Research in Social Work Practice* 8:657–667.

Rothman, David J. 1980. *Conscience and convenience: The asylum and its alternatives in progressive America.* Glenview, Illinois: Scott, Foresman and Company.

Sanborn, Joseph B., Jr. 1998. Second-class justice, first-class punishment: The use of juvenile records in sentencing adults. *Judicature* 81 (5): 206–213.

———. 1993. The right to a public jury trial: A need for today's juvenile court. *Judicature* 76:230–238.

Schlossman, Steven L. 1977. *Love and the American delinquent.* Chicago: University of Chicago Press.

Schlossman, Steven L., and Stephanie Wallach. 1978. The crime of precocious sexuality: Female juvenile delinquency in the Progressive Era. *Harvard Educational Review* 48:65–94.

Schur, Edwin M. 1971. *Labeling deviant behavior: Its sociological implications.* New York: Harper & Row.

Shine, James, and Dwight Price. 1992. Prosecutors and juvenile justice: New roles and perspectives. In *Juvenile justice and public policy: Toward a national agenda*, edited by I.M. Schwartz. New York: Lexington Books.

Singer, Simon I. 1996. *Recriminalizing delinquency: Violent juvenile crime and juvenile justice reform.* Cambridge: Cambridge University Press.

Singer, Simon I., and David McDowall. 1988. Criminalizing delinquency: The deterrent effects of the New York juvenile offender law. *Law & Society Review* 22:521–535.

Snyder, Howard, Terrence Finnegan, Anne Stahl, and Rowen Poole. 1998. *Easy access to juvenile court statistics: 1987–1996* (data presentation and analysis package). Pittsburgh: National Center for Juvenile Justice (producer). Washington, D.C.: U.S. Department of Justice, Office of Juvenile Justice and Delinquency Prevention (distributor).

Snyder, Howard, and Melissa Sickmund. 1999. *Juvenile offenders and victims: 1999 National Report.* Report, NCJ 178257. Washington, D.C.: U.S. Department of Justice, Office of Juvenile Justice and Delinquency Prevention.

———. 1995. *Juvenile offenders and victims: A national report.* NCJ 153569. Washington, D.C.: U.S. Department of Justice, Office of Juvenile Justice and Delinquency Prevention.

Snyder, Howard, Melissa Sickmund, and Eileen Poe-Yamagata. 1999. *The conversion of juvenile delinquents to adult criminals: Four studies of juvenile transfers to criminal court in the 1990s.* Pittsburgh: National Center for Juvenile Justice.

Springer, Charles E. 1991. Rehabilitating the juvenile court. *Notre Dame Journal of Law, Ethics & Public Policy* 5:397–420.

Stahl, Anne L. 1999. *Offenders in juvenile court, 1996.* Juvenile Justice Bulletin, NCJ 175719. Washington, D.C.: U.S. Department of Justice, Office of Juvenile Justice and Delinquency Prevention.

Sutton, John R. 1988. *Stubborn children: Controlling delinquency in the United States.* Berkeley: University of California Press.

Tonry, Michael. 1996. *Sentencing matters.* New York: Oxford University Press.

Torbet, Patricia, and Linda Szymanski. 1998. *State legislative responses to violent juvenile crime: 1996–97 update.* Juvenile Justice Bulletin, NCJ 172835. Washington, D.C.: U.S. Department of Justice, Office of Juvenile Justice and Delinquency Prevention.

Torbet, Patricia, Richard Gable, Hunter Hurst IV, Imogene Montgomery, Linda Szymanski, and Douglas Thomas. 1996. *State responses to serious and violent juvenile crime*. Research Report, NCJ 161565. Washington, D.C.: U.S. Department of Justice, Office of Juvenile Justice and Delinquency Prevention.

U.S. Bureau of the Census. 1999. Population estimates for the U.S. and States by single year of age and sex: July 1, 1996. Doc. no. ST–98–12. Retrieved 8 February 2000 from the World Wide Web: http://www.census.gov/population/estimates/state/stats/ag9698.txt.

U.S. General Accounting Office. 1995. *Juvenile justice: Juveniles processed in criminal court and case dispositions*. Washington, D.C.

U.S. Senate. [1927] 1974. *Message from the President of the United States, transmitting a letter from the judge of the Juvenile Court of the District of Columbia, submitting a report covering the work of the Juvenile Court during the period from July 1, 1906 to June 30, 1926*. Reprinted in *Metropolitan America*. New York: Arno Press.

Watkins, John C., Jr. 1998. *The juvenile justice century*. Durham, North Carolina: Carolina Academic Press.

Winner, Lawrence, Lonn Lanza-Kaduce, Donna M. Bishop, and Charles E. Frazier. 1997. The transfer of juveniles to criminal court: Reexamining recidivism over the long term. *Crime & Delinquency* 43:548–563.

Wyden, Ron. 1997. Senator Wyden of Oregon, floor speech. S. 10, 105th Cong., 1st Sess. *Congressional Record*, 17 March, vol. 143, no. 34.

Zimring, Franklin E. 1991. The treatment of hard cases in American juvenile justice: In defense of discretionary waiver. *Notre Dame Journal of Law, Ethics & Public Policy* 5:267–280.

www.ingramcontent.com/pod-product-compliance
Lightning Source LLC
Chambersburg PA
CBHW070121010626

45794CB00012B/1145